Modern Language Assoc

D0910984

Approaches to Teaching
World Literature

Joseph Gibaldi, Series Editor

29. Richard K. Emmerson, ed. *Approaches to Teaching Medieval English Drama.* 1990.
30. Kathleen Blake, ed. *Approaches to Teaching Eliot's* Middlemarch. 1990.
31. María Elena de Valdés and Mario J. Valdés, eds. *Approaches to Teaching García Márquez's* One Hundred Years of Solitude. 1990.
32. Donald D. Kummings, ed. *Approaches to Teaching Whitman's* Leaves of Grass. 1990.
33. Stephen C. Behrendt, ed. *Approaches to Teaching Shelley's* Frankenstein. 1990.
34. June Schlueter and Enoch Brater, eds. *Approaches to Teaching Beckett's* Waiting for Godot. 1991.
35. Walter H. Evert and Jack W. Rhodes, eds. *Approaches to Teaching Keats's Poetry.* 1991

Approaches to Teaching Keats's Poetry

Edited by

Walter H. Evert

and

Jack W. Rhodes

The Modern Language Association of America
New York   1991

Library of Congress Cataloging-in-Publication Data

Approaches to teaching Keats's poetry / edited by Walter H. Evert and
 Jack W. Rhodes.
   p. cm.—(Approaches to teaching world literature ; 35)
   Includes bibliographical references and index.
   ISBN 0-87352-543-4 (cloth)   ISBN 0-87352-544-2 (paper)
   1. Keats, John, 1795–1821—Criticism and interpretation.
   2. Keats, John, 1795–1821—Study and teaching.   I. Evert, Walter H.
   II. Rhodes, Jack Wright.   III. Series.
   PR4837.A64   1991
   821'.7—dc20   91-10863

Cover illustration of the paperback edition: Raphael, *A Knight's Dream*,
National Gallery, London, c. 1505. Photograph: Alinari/Art Resource.

Published by The Modern Language Association of America
10 Astor Place, New York, New York 10003-6981

CONTENTS

PREFACE TO THE SERIES

In *The Art of Teaching* Gilbert Highet wrote, "Bad teaching wastes a great deal of effort, and spoils many lives which might have been full of energy and happiness." All too many teachers have failed in their work, Highet argued, simply "because they have not thought about it." We hope that the Approaches to Teaching World Literature series, sponsored by the Modern Language Association's Publications Committee, will not only improve the craft—as well as the art—of teaching but also encourage serious and continuing discussion of the aims and methods of teaching literature.

The principal objective of the series is to collect within each volume different points of view on teaching a specific literary work, a literary tradition, or a writer widely taught at the undergraduate level. The preparation of each volume begins with a wide-ranging survey of instructors, thus enabling us to include in the volume the philosophies and approaches, thoughts and methods of scores of experienced teachers. The result is a sourcebook of material, information, and ideas on teaching the subject of the volume to undergraduates.

The series is intended to serve nonspecialists as well as specialists, inexperienced as well as experienced teachers, graduate students who wish to learn effective ways of teaching as well as senior professors who wish to compare their own approaches with the approaches of colleagues in other schools. Of course, no volume in the series can ever substitute for erudition, intelligence, creativity, and sensitivity in teaching. We hope merely that each book will point readers in useful directions; at most each will offer only a first step in the long journey to successful teaching.

Joseph Gibaldi
Series Editor

PREFACE TO THE VOLUME

The reasons for devoting a volume in this series to the teaching of Keats's poetry are not far to seek. The series is intended primarily to serve the teachers of undergraduates, and few poets are as congenial to undergraduates as Keats. Much of his poetry was written when he was the students' own age, and the urgencies and perplexities of that time in life are often communicated in his poetry with frank and fresh immediacy. He is "easy to read" in the sense that his vocabulary and syntax are essentially our own; and, while he is deeply thoughtful, most of his poetry can be satisfactorily understood without the historical freight of politics, philosophy, theology, or the other arcana that enrich but also encumber the study of much non-contemporary literature. The shortness and difficulty of Keats's life add poignancy to a study of his poetry, and the small body of his work makes him more comprehensively assimilable than most other poets. Finally, he comes through to the reader as a good person, socially gregarious, high-minded without being sententious, personally modest, of ingenuous character and ameliorative bent. He is taught in high school and in graduate school; and in undergraduate college programs he is taught in everything from Introduction to Literature and Survey of British Literature courses to Romanticism surveys and senior seminars, either alone or paired with one of his major contemporaries or, more broadly, with such noncontiguous figures as Shakespeare and Wallace Stevens. He is everywhere in the curriculum.

That in itself does not ensure, of course, that he is always transparently accessible. As some of our contributors point out, the students' cognitive complacency is usually premature—there is more there than at first meets the eye—and we do, after all, engage his poetry with an experience of both literature and the world that differs from his own. And to speak of difference is not to speak of merely contingent change. If it is true that, excepting the electronics revolution, all the instrumentalities that have forged our contemporary society were already in place during Keats's lifetime, it is also true that their development and implementation have created modes of awareness and concern that he could never have imagined, even in the study of literature. That being so, it is well to turn to colleagues who have met the challenge of teaching him, in a wide variety of modes, as we take up the task ourselves.

Toward that end we have provided a bibliography of texts, reference works, background readings, and critical studies that the respondents to our questionnaire have found useful, supplemented with a few others that we thought it desirable to include. We have made no attempt to produce a complete listing of all existing works, or even of all potentially useful works, concerning Romanticism and Keats. We include references to bibliographical resources that will provide many hundreds of pages of further information, hoping meanwhile that the materials recommended by our respondents will be sufficient to provide a solid substructure of information and ideas. A further perusal of the Works Cited section at the end of the volume will provide an even fuller, and certainly more eclectic, range of references, including not only an alphabetized reordering of the "Materials" section but also additional works that the contributors to the "Approaches" section found useful in the preparation of their essays. The "Approaches" section provides examples of classroom strategies, theoretical perspectives, and unifying themes that the writers have used successfully in teaching Keats's poetry. None of the essays, even the most theoretical, is without a practical classroom dimension.

In addition to these now traditional components of the series volumes, we begin with a "Brief Handlist" of works to orient the new teacher; we also provide sections called "Keats's Works Assigned" and "Papers and Other Assignments." These latter sections list the poems and letters most frequently taught by our respondents and include a selection of actual writing assignments. We hope the example of a few written exercises that have already been tried might be a helpful stimulus to the beginning teacher's own or adaptive ideas. In addition, there is an index to the most frequently treated topics in Keats's letters and, for the person who is interested less in a single orientation than in what the contributors have to say about a particular poem, a title and first-line index of the poems.

We wish to thank the Citadel Development Foundation, without whose generous support this book would not have been possible. Our gratitude is also due to Laura Norman for her diligent help with proofreading; to Jean Rhyne, of the Thomas Cooper Library of the University of South Carolina; and to Sherman Pyatt, Herbert Nath, Betsy Carter, Ed Maynard, and Zelma Palestrant, of the Daniel Library of The Citadel. Thanks, too, to Jean Rucks Rhodes, whose help has been invaluable in too many ways to name, and to Evan and Emma Rhodes, whose forbearance with an inexplicably occupied father remains to be repaid.

We wish finally to thank the respondents to our questionnaire and, in additional measure, those who volunteered to write essays, all of whom are truly the only begetters of the volume. Inevitably, the demand for representativeness and the limitations of space prevented our using all the essays so generously offered, but our task was made easier for having had such an abundance to choose from. We wish also to thank Robert F. Gleckner and Spencer Hall, who more or less by accident found themselves in a position to offer practical advice gained from their experience as editors of other volumes in this series. And finally, of course, we must express our gratitude to Joseph Gibaldi, the series editor, for his patience and his almost magical ability to be available for instant consultation at virtually any hour of any day, and also to his editorial committee and their consultants, none of whom is known to us but who collectively kept us on course at each of the project's decisive stages.

WHE and JWR

Part One

MATERIALS

Brief Handlist

The pages that follow contain a substantial accounting of the informational resources concerning Keats and his texts, his thought and artistry, and the intellectual world of which he is a part. These few lines are for those who would like a more compact orientation. The standard edition of Keats's poetry is the one edited by Jack Stillinger in two different formats (1978 and 1982—consult the following pages and the Works Cited section at the back of this volume for fuller information on this and other works mentioned here). The edition with the fullest and most helpful annotations is Miriam Allott's. The standard edition of Keats's letters is that edited by Hyder Edward Rollins, which also contains in the first of its two volumes a full chronology of Keats's life and biographical sketches of most of his friends and associates. Lilian R. Furst's little volume *Romanticism* provides a compact essay on the characteristics of pan-European Romanticism; and, if one has an hour or so for browsing, her *European Romanticism: Self-Definition* is a delightful (and ultimately probably subversive) anthology of definitions of the key terms by virtually all the actual players in the game. For a brief, but thoughtful and thorough, introduction to Keats's poetry, preceded by a sufficient biographical section, we recommend Wolf Z. Hirst's *John Keats*; but if that should not be available, Douglas Bush's *John Keats: His Life and Writings* is a longtime favorite, and John Barnard's *John Keats* is concise and pithy. Among comprehensive critical studies of the past twenty years, Stuart M. Sperry's *Keats the Poet* has been a standard reference, rooted in mainstream criticism but pointing the way to much that has become central in the revisionary criticism of the years since its publication.

Texts

Among the anthologies of Romantic writing, David Perkins's *English Romantic Writers* is the most widely used. It provides a generous selection of the poems, plus thirty-six letters, in addition to some significant ancillary material, such as passages from J. G. Lockhart's "On the Cockney School of Poetry" and from Charles Cowden Clarke's *Recollections of Writers*. The chief limitation of this book is that, unrevised (at the time of this writing) since 1967, the bibliographies and commentaries are limited to the structures of thought current at that time. John L. Mahoney's *English Romantics* has only half as many poems, omits *Endymion* entirely, and prints only eight letters but does include significant essays on Keats by Cleanth Brooks, Earl Wasserman, and Stuart Sperry. Harold Bloom and Lionel Trilling's *Romantic Poetry and Prose* offers twenty-one poems (about the same as Mahoney) and fourteen letters. This work is the Romantics section of the *Oxford Anthology of English Literature* printed paperbound. Finally, William Heath's *Major British Poets of the Romantic Period* contains all the best-known poems complete (except for *Endymion*, which is represented only by book 1) and a liberal selection of sonnets and lesser-known poems, but only eighteen of the letters, several excerpted. For Survey of British Literature courses, the standard text is *The Norton Anthology of English Literature* (Abrams), the Keats section of which is edited by Jack Stillinger. Some teachers use this text to teach even upper-level courses in Romanticism, since it contains about the same number of poems and letters as either Mahoney or Bloom and Trilling, includes at least a couple of pages of *Endymion*, has an excellent general introduction to Keats, and provides a helpful bibliography at the end. George K. Anderson, William E. Buckler, and Mary Harris Veeder's *Literature of England* may also be useful for its visual materials.

The standard edition of Keats's poetry, now and surely for at least a generation to come, is Jack Stillinger's *Poems of John Keats* (1978). The student edition, *John Keats: Complete Poems*, has the same text but a simplified apparatus, reduced textual notes, and added glosses. The concordance based on Stillinger's 1978 text is Michael G. Becker, Robert J. Dilligan, and Todd K. Bender's *Concordance to the Poems of John Keats*. Because Stillinger prints the poems in chronological order of composition, some people find it useful to consult the previous "standard" text, H. W. Garrod's *Poetical Works of John Keats*, which presents the poems in the order of their first collected, or posthumous, publication. While this arrangement can answer certain questions more readily than a chronological one can, Garrod's text is no longer considered authoritative for purposes of scholarly citation, so that, the question answered, one reverts to Stillinger for accuracy of quotation. While also lacking final textual authority, Miriam Allott's *Poems of John Keats* is by far the most fully annotated edition and would be the volume of choice for students interested in echoes of other poets, recurrences within the body of Keats's poetry, allusions to classical myth and story, definitions of unusual words, and the like. In addition to Stillinger's, other paperback texts of complete or selected works available at the time of this writing include editions by John Barnard, Philip Levine, George H. Ford, and H. W. Garrod. None has the authority of Stillinger, but, where price is a consideration, one of these might be found practicable. Although now out of print, the 1966 Signet paperback *John Keats: Selected Poetry* is worthwhile tracking down because of the introduction by Paul de Man. Among our respondents who use paperbacks, the text of choice remains, overwhelmingly, Douglas Bush's *John Keats: Selected Poems and Letters*, which contains all the best-known poems and letters, including the complete *Endymion*.

The standard edition of Keats's letters is Hyder Edward Rollins's two-volume *Letters of John Keats, 1814–1821*. Robert Gittings's *Letters of John Keats: A New Selection*, available in paperback, eliminates some seventy of the least consequential letters but corrects Rollins in some interesting particulars. H. Buxton Forman and Maurice Buxton Forman's eight-volume *Poetical Works and Other Writings of John Keats*, superseded by all the above, nevertheless retains interest for its inclusion of marginalia and occasional writings not readily available elsewhere.

Donald H. Reiman is the general editor of a series of texts being published under the title *The Manuscripts of the Younger Romantics: A Facsimile Edition, with Scholarly Introductions, Bibliographical Descriptions, and Annotations*. The intent of these is to take us back, beyond even the standard editions of the moment, to the point of immediate apprehension of the poet's writing hand and mind, so that we can eliminate editorial intervention and draw our own inferences about authorial intentions and renderings. While these texts are not for every student, most should be capable of curious glances at them, and those who seek them out are probably next in line to take our places. In 1985 the first four volumes of Keats materials appeared, edited by Jack Stillinger: 1, Poems *(1817): A Facsimile of Richard Woodhouse's Annotated Copy in the Huntington Library*; 2, Endymion: *A Facsimile of the Revised Holograph Manuscript*; 3, Endymion *(1818): A Facsimile of Richard Woodhouse's Annotated Copy in the Berg Collection*; and 4, *Poems, Transcripts, Letters, Etc.: Facsimiles of Richard Woodhouse's Scrapbook Materials in the Pierpont Morgan Library*. Volume 5 came out in 1989: *Manuscript Poems in the British Library*; and two succeeding volumes appeared in 1988: 6, *The Woodhouse Poetry Transcripts at Harvard, a Facsimile of the Wðpð2 Notebook, with Description and Contents of the Wðpð1 Notebook*; 7, *The Charles Brown Poetry Transcripts at Harvard, Facsimiles including the Fair Copy of* Otho the Great. Although most of the material here—manuscripts by and about Keats, biographical and textual annotations of Keats's works—has been reproduced by or incorporated in modern scholarship, these volumes provide, in a way scholarship cannot, an immediate sense of Keats's daily literary activity.

Biographies

Keats studies is fortunate in its number of excellent biographies. Two appeared in 1963: Walter Jackson Bate's *John Keats* and Aileen Ward's *John*

Keats: The Making of a Poet. Each is outstanding in a different way: Bate for his criticism and Ward for her psychological insight. In 1968 a third worthy biography was added, Robert Gittings's *John Keats*, which has the virtue of being more factually detailed than the other two. Older biographies that still have merit are Sidney Colvin's *John Keats: His Life and Poetry, His Friends, Critics, and After-Fame*, an astute volume having the interest of critical predications not our own; Amy Lowell's *John Keats*, in which an acute poetic mind is brought to bear on historical sources; and Dorothy Hewlett's *Adonais: A Life of John Keats*, a straightforward account not freighted with scholarly subtleties. For reliable and comprehensive biographies conceived on a more introductory scale than the above, see Douglas Bush's *John Keats: His Life and Writings* and Wolf Z. Hirst's *John Keats*, the latter chiefly concerned with the poet's creative life. Timothy Hilton's *Keats and His World* is a popular, unpretentious, and very well illustrated introduction to the life. A student interested in the development of Keats's reputation or in a compact case study of biography as social history might be sent to William Henry Marquess's *Lives of the Poet: The First Century of Keats Biography*.

A good deal of primary biographical material is interesting and useful for its immediacy and its occasional contextual implications. Among the most readily available are the letters, in both the Rollins and the Gittings editions; Rollins's *Keats Circle: Letters and Papers*, which includes documents and letters concerning Keats written by his friends and associates; the earliest biographical sketch, Dorothy Hyde Bodurtha and Willard Bissell Pope's edition of Life of John Keats *by Charles Armitage Brown*, also included in the previous Rollins item; Leonidas M. Jones's *Letters of John Hamilton Reynolds*; Jack Stillinger's edition of *The Letters of Charles Armitage Brown*; Charles Cowden Clarke and Mary Cowden Clarke's *Recollections of Writers*, in which a schoolmaster, and later friend, of the poet recalls Keats's early character and interests; J. E. Morpurgo's edition of *The Autobiography of Leigh Hunt*, which gives Hunt's side of a friendship that eventually caused distress on both sides; Willard Bissell Pope's five-volume edition of *The Diary of Benjamin Robert Haydon*; and the publication that is credited with establishing Keats as a poet to be taken seriously, the two-volume *Life, Letters, and Literary Remains of John Keats* by Lord Houghton (Richard Monckton Milnes). Periodical reviews, in Keats's time, of his work and the works of his principal associates have been gathered together in the last two volumes of Donald H. Reiman's nine-volume *Romantics Reviewed: Contemporary Reviews of British Romantic Writers*. Convenient thumbnail sketches of most of Keats's friends and correspondents (not always easy to track down otherwise) can be found in Rollins's *Letters* and *Keats Circle*. The first volume of the *Letters* also has a detailed chronology (now perhaps correctable in isolated particulars) of the major events in Keats's life.

Readings in Romanticism

For a general understanding of Romanticism at book length, in roughly chronological order and with the emphases indicated in their titles or appended comments, one might consult Mario Praz's *Romantic Agony*, which stresses the emotional extremes of Romanticism; Douglas Bush's *Mythology and the Romantic Tradition*; G. Wilson Knight's *Starlit Dome: Studies in the Poetry of Vision*, which analyzes how four major Romantics, in images and symbols, deal with themes of eternity; Walter Jackson Bate's *From Classic to Romantic* and, as background, his *Burden of the Past*; D. G. James's *Romantic Comedy*, which examines how the Romantics used myth in their Christian and spiritual struggles; Cecil M. Bowra's *Romantic Imagination*; M. H. Abrams's *Mirror and the Lamp*, which traces the development of Romantic literary theory from eighteenth-century antecedents, and his *Natural Supernaturalism*, which analyzes the secularization of religious motives in the Romantic period; volume 2 of René Wellek's *History of Modern Criticism, 1750–1950*; Robert Langbaum's *Poetry of Experience: The Dramatic Monologue in Modern Literary Tradition*; David Perkins's *Quest for Permanence*, which explores the Romantic theme of yearning for stability and permanence; Jacques Barzun's *Classic, Romantic, and Modern*; Harold Bloom's *Visionary Company: A Reading of English Romantic Poetry*, which analyzes the interplay between imagination (and internal states) and actuality (and external ones) in Romantic poetry (for an extension of the imagination into a less controlled but more determinative force, see Bloom's *Poetry and Repression*); Morse Peckham's *Beyond the Tragic Vision*, which sees Romanticism as replacing the value of the tragic vision with the struggle for value itself, and his *Triumph of Romanticism*, a collection of essays on various aspects of Romantic theory and culture; Edward Bostetter's *Romantic Ventriloquists*, which examines Romantic poets' discomfort with the truths of their own oracular voices; Martin Price's *To the Palace of Wisdom*, which provides a history of the eighteenth-century idea of order, important for an understanding of Romanticism; Brian Wilkie's *Romantic Poets and Epic Tradition*; Karl Kroeber's *Romantic Narrative Art*; Northrop Frye's *Study of English Romanticism*; Lilian R. Furst's *Romanticism in Perspective*; Geoffrey Hartman's *Beyond Formalism*, which puts Romantic antianalyticism into a nonformalist perspective in a series of essays on topics ranging from Malraux to Robert Lowell; Donald A. Low's *That Sunny Dome: A Portrait of Regency England*; Michael Ragussis's *Subterfuge of Art: Language and the Romantic Tradition*, which presents, in a Lawrentian perspective, a Freudian analysis of the Romantic distrust of the truth of words and the literature they form; Hugh Honour's *Romanticism*, which surveys Romanticism in the visual arts; Anne K. Mellor's *English Romantic Irony*; Michael G. Cooke's *Acts of In-*

clusion: Studies Bearing on an Elementary Theory of Romanticism, which examines universality as characteristic of Romanticism; Tilottama Rajan's *Dark Interpreter: The Discourse of Romanticism*, which deconstructs Romantic affirmation as a conscious and conservative backing-away from modernist conclusions; James Engell's *Creative Imagination*, which views the Romantic imagination as a creation of the eighteenth century; John Clubbe and Ernest J. Lovell's *English Romanticism: The Grounds of Belief*, which stresses unity of thought among Romantic writers; Jerome McGann's *Romantic Ideology: A Critical Investigation*, which charges criticism and scholarship of Romanticism with basing its judgments on a set of values itself Romantic and goes on to employ a more strict sociohistorical analysis; Peter L. Thorslev's *Romantic Contraries: Freedom versus Destiny*, in which all the permutations of the title's dichotomy are examined as determinants of Romantic thought; Nancy Moore Goslee's *Uriel's Eye: Miltonic Stationing and Statuary in Blake, Keats, and Shelley*; Stuart Curran's *Poetic Form and British Romanticism*, a thorough survey of Romantic works in terms of genres and their adaptations; Morris Eaves and Michael Fischer's *Romanticism and Contemporary Criticism*, conference papers by major figures, pro and con the title topic, much illuminated by the transcript of a prolonged question-and-answer session afterward; Lore Metzger's *One Foot in Eden: Modes of Pastoral in Romantic Poetry*, in which chapters 7 and 8 deal specifically with Keats's adaptations of pastoral topoi in "Hyperion" and the odes; Donald Reiman's *Intervals of Inspiration: The Skeptical Tradition and the Psychology of Romanticism*; and Marilyn Gaull's *English Romanticism: The Human Context*, which presents "historical, social, cultural, political, economic, intellectual, philosophical, artistic, and scientific backgrounds" of Romantic literature.

Early essays on the nature of Romanticism have made major contributions to our understanding of the phenomenon and warrant study. There have been many, but some of the most important are A. O. Lovejoy's "IX. The Temporalizing of the Chain of Being" and "X. Romanticism and the Principle of Plenitude" in *The Great Chain of Being* and his "On the Discrimination of Romanticisms"; René Wellek's "Concept of 'Romanticism' in Literary History"; and Morse Peckham's "Toward a Theory of Romanticism" and "Toward a Theory of Romanticism II: Reconsiderations." These are supplemented by Northrop Frye's "Drunken Boat: The Revolutionary Element in Romanticism" in *Romanticism Reconsidered*; M. H. Abrams's "Structure and Style in the Greater Romantic Lyric"; and, more recently, Hans Eichner's "Rise of Modern Science and the Genesis of Romanticism."

General Background and Reference Works

Reference works and background materials abound that are useful to the beginning teacher of Keats. Anthologies of influential eighteenth-century writings inform about currents of thought Keats might have been swimming either with or against: Leonard M. Trawick's *Backgrounds of Romanticism: English Philosophical Prose of the Eighteenth Century*, Karl Kroeber's *Backgrounds to British Romantic Literature*, and Brian Hepworth's *Rise of Romanticism: Essential Texts*. For historical studies of the period, see G. M. Trevelyan's *British History of the Nineteenth Century and After (1782–1919)*, Élie Halévy's *England in 1815*, Asa Briggs's *Making of Modern England: 1783–1867*, and R. J. White's *Life in Regency England* and *From Waterloo to Peterloo*. Some useful historical surveys of the literature of the period are William L. Renwick's *English Literature, 1789–1815* and Ian Jack's *English Literature, 1815–1832* (vols. 9 and 10 in the *Oxford History of English Literature*), Oliver Elton's *Survey of English Literature, 1780–1830*, and J. R. de J. Jackson's *Poetry of the Romantic Period*. For the perspective of Romantic poetry *within* history, see Carl Woodring's *Politics in English Romantic Poetry*, A. D. Harvey's *English Poetry in a Changing Society, 1780–1825*, and Marilyn Butler's *Romantics, Rebels, and Reactionaries*.

The primary journals relevant to Keats are the *Keats-Shelley Journal*, *Studies in Romanticism*, *Wordsworth Circle*, the Fall issue of *Studies in English Literature*, *Nineteenth Century Studies*, and *Nineteenth Century Contexts* (published before 1987 under the title *Romanticism Past and Present*). Access to some of the periodical literature concerning Romanticism is made more convenient through collections of essays: *Romanticism: Points of View*, edited by Robert F. Gleckner and Gerald E. Enscoe (which exists in two quite different editions, 1962 and 1970); *Romanticism Reconsidered: Selected Papers from the English Institute*, edited by Northrop Frye; *Romanticism and Consciousness*, edited by Harold Bloom; *The Romantics*, edited by Stephen Prickett; and *Romanticism: Vistas, Instances, Continuities*, edited by David Thorburn and Geoffrey Hartman.

There are several bibliographies to consult regarding John Keats and the Romantic period. The annual *MLA International Bibliography*, of course, covers both fields and many others as well. Donald H. Reiman's *English Romantic Poetry, 1800–1835*, published in 1979, has a chapter on Keats and treats other useful topics, including background studies covering social, economic, political, intellectual, artistic, and literary history. Walter Graham began "The Romantic Movement: A Selective and Critical Bibliography" in *ELH* in 1937; over the years it has become closely associated with David Erdman, who began working on it in 1948. In 1950 it moved to *Philological*

Quarterly and in 1965 to *English Language Notes.* Beginning in 1979 it has been published as an annual under the same title by Garland Publishing. Since 1952, the *Keats-Shelley Journal* has published "Current Bibliography," now compiled by Clement Dunbar, which includes a section on Keats as well as one on English Romanticism. Both Erdman's and Dunbar's bibliographies provide helpful annotations. A. C. Elkins, Jr., and L. J. Forstner have gathered Erdman's work in *The Romantic Movement Bibliography, 1936–1970: A Master Cumulation* in seven volumes. The bibliography of the *Keats-Shelley Journal* has been gathered in David Bonnell Green and Edwin Graves Wilson's *Keats, Shelley, Byron, Hunt, and Their Circles: A Bibliography: July 1, 1950–June 30, 1962* and in Robert A. Hartley's *Keats, Shelley, Byron, Hunt, and Their Circles: A Bibliography: July 1, 1962– December 31, 1974.* Three annual reviews of scholarship will provide a convenient, if selective, overview of recent work: *The Year's Work in English Studies,* the Modern Humanities Research Association's *Annual Bibliography of English Language and Literature,* and the Autumn number of *Studies in English Literature,* which focuses on nineteenth-century English literature.

The earliest thorough bibliography of Keats published as a book is J. R. MacGillivray's *Keats: A Bibliography and Reference Guide.* Richard Harter Fogle's Goldentree series *Romantic Poets and Prose Writers* is a handy tool, updated by Ronald B. Hearn's *Keats Criticism since 1954.* There is also Jack Wright Rhodes's more specialized *Keats's Major Odes: An Annotated Bibliography of the Criticism.* More useful than any of these, however, for gaining a background in Keats scholarship, is Frank Jordan's *English Romantic Poets: A Review of Research and Criticism,* which covers Romanticism plus the major Romantic poets. Readers will benefit both from Clarence D. Thorpe and David Perkins's chapter on Keats in the third edition of this work and from Jack Stillinger's in the fourth. The differences between the two treatments will provide a quick perspective on Keats criticism.

Reviews of books about Keats and other Romantic topics appear in the Autumn issue of the *Wordsworth Circle* (previously, 1973–84, in the Summer issue), every issue of the *Keats-Shelley Journal, Studies in Romanticism, Romanticism Past and Present* (retrospectively through 1986), the Fall issue of *Studies in English Literature,* and *The Romantic Movement: A Selective and Critical Bibliography* (for both books and major articles). Also, pertinent reviews can frequently be found in *Criticism, Journal of English and Germanic Philology, Nineteenth Century Literature,* and other periodicals.

Keats has attracted the critical attention of many of the most talented readers since his time, which is a measure of his greatness. And, considering the brevity of his canon, the quantity of criticism about him is remarkable. A basic knowledge for teachers of Keats might begin at book length with

G. M. Matthews's *Keats: The Critical Heritage* for a survey of the responses to Keats from the time of his first publication up through 1863. Also, early reviews of Keats's poetry are reprinted in Donald Reiman's *Romantics Reviewed*. Then, in order of publication beginning in 1880, are Frances M. Owen's *John Keats*; Robert Bridges's *John Keats: A Critical Essay*; John Middleton Murry's *Keats and Shakespeare*; H. W. Garrod's *Keats*; Clarence D. Thorpe's *Mind of John Keats*; M. R. Ridley's *Keats' Craftsmanship: A Study in Poetic Development*; Claude Lee Finney's *Evolution of Keats's Poetry*; Lawrence John Zillman's *John Keats and the Sonnet Tradition*; Walter Jackson Bate's *Stylistic Development of Keats*; James Ralston Caldwell's *John Keats' Fancy: The Effect on Keats of the Psychology of His Day*; Richard Harter Fogle's *Imagery of Keats and Shelley: A Comparative Study*; Newell F. Ford's *Prefigurative Imagination of John Keats: A Study of the Beauty-Truth Identification and Its Implications*; Earl R. Wasserman's *Finer Tone: Keats' Major Poems*; Robert Gittings's *John Keats: The Living Year*; Murry's *Keats*; Gittings's *Mask of Keats: A Study of Problems*; E. C. Pettet's *On the Poetry of Keats*; Bernice Slote's *Keats and the Dramatic Principle*; Bernard Blackstone's *Consecrated Urn: An Interpretation of Keats in Terms of Growth and Form*; Walter H. Evert's *Aesthetic and Myth in the Poetry of Keats*; Mario L. D'Avanzo's *Keats's Metaphors for the Poetic Imagination*; Ian Jack's *Keats and the Mirror of Art*; John Jones's *John Keats's Dream of Truth*; Gerald B. Kauvar's *Other Poetry of Keats*; M. A. Goldberg's *Poetics of Romanticism: Toward a Reading of John Keats*; Charles I. Patterson's *Daemonic in the Poetry of John Keats*; Morris Dickstein's *Keats and His Poetry: A Study in Development*; Jack Stillinger's *Hoodwinking of Madeline and Other Essays on Keats's Poems*; Stuart M. Sperry's *Keats the Poet*; Christopher Ricks's *Keats and Embarrassment*; James Land Jones's *Adam's Dream: Mythic Consciousness in Keats and Yeats*; Judy Little's *Keats as a Narrative Poet: A Test of Invention*; Stuart A. Ende's *Keats and the Sublime*; Robert M. Ryan's *Keats: The Religious Sense*; Ronald A. Sharp's *Keats, Skepticism, and the Religion of Beauty*; Barry Gradman's *Metamorphosis in Keats*; Helen Vendler's *Odes of John Keats*; Dorothy Van Ghent's *Keats: The Myth of the Hero*; Donald C. Goellnicht's *Poet-Physician: Keats and Medical Science*; Martin Aske's *Keats and Hellenism*; Leon Waldoff's *Keats and the Silent Work of Imagination*; Susan J. Wolfson's *Questioning Presence: Wordsworth, Keats, and the Interrogative Mode in Romantic Poetry*; and John Barnard's *John Keats* (1987).

Several collections of essays provide convenient access to some of the most important periodical literature, both original and reprinted: *Keats' Well-Read Urn*, edited by Harvey T. Lyon; *John Keats: A Reassessment*, edited by Kenneth Muir; *Keats: A Collection of Critical Essays*, edited by Walter Jackson Bate; *Critics on Keats*, edited by Judith O'Neill; *Twentieth-Century*

Interpretations of Keats's Odes, edited by Jack Stillinger; *Twentieth-Century Interpretations of "The Eve of St. Agnes,"* edited by Alan Danzig; and *The Odes of Keats*, edited by Harold Bloom.

Finally, since Keats was such a diligent student of literature and literary craftsmanship, a truly comprehensive understanding of his poetry requires a knowledge of the things he read. The four poets most significant for Keats were Chaucer, Spenser, Shakespeare, and Milton, though he was interested, too, in the Bible, Homer, Vergil, Ovid, Dante (H. F. Cary's 1814 translation), Tasso (Edward Fairfax's 1600 translation), and Ariosto. He also knew Sophocles, Petrarch (John Nott's 1808 translation), Burton's *Anatomy of Melancholy*, Jonson, Beaumont and Fletcher, *Palmerin of England* (Robert Southey's 1817 translation), the *Spectator*, Lucius Apuleius's *Golden Ass* (William Adlington's 1566 translation), William Beckford's *Vathek* (1786), Thomas Chatterton, John Dryden, William Godwin, Pope, Sheridan, Smollett, Sterne, and Swift. In addition, he found ideas and information in John Lemprière's *Classical Dictionary* (1788), John Potter's *Archaeologia Graeca* (1697, 1699), John Bonnycastle's *Introduction to Astronomy* (1807), Andrew Tooke's *Pantheon* (1698), Gilbert Burnet's *History of His Own Time* (1809), William Robertson's *History of America* (1777) and *History of Scotland* (1759), and Joseph Spence's *Polymetis* (1747). He was acquainted with some French writers as well, such as Corneille, Rabelais, Ronsard, Rousseau, Molière, and Voltaire, though his embrace of foreign literatures was measured: "I shall never become attach'd to a foreign idiom so as to put it into my writings" (Rollins, *Letters* 2: 212).

Among his contemporaries, Keats was most interested in Hazlitt, Coleridge, and Wordsworth. He was also familiar with the work of Walter Scott, Leigh Hunt, Shelley, Byron, and others. His reading of contemporary periodicals most often included *Blackwood's, Annals of the Fine Arts, Edinburgh Review, Quarterly Review, Examiner,* and *London Magazine.* Keats drew much of his inspiration and tried to develop his art, perhaps more consciously than many other writers, in response to the models provided by the great works of literature past. Moreover, he tended to see himself, even late in his brief career, as an apprentice poet with much to learn. Thus, he read keenly and studiously. Teachers of Keats will understand his attempts at poetic growth more clearly by bearing in mind the authors and works he adopted as presiding spirits.

Audiovisual Resources

The significance for Keats of the visual arts has been demonstrated ably by Ian Jack and others. (See the essay by Nicholas O. Warner in this volume.)

While many teachers of English do not feel comfortable spending much time in their classes on the fine arts because they have not been formally prepared to do so, students find it interesting and enlivening if a course includes some visual help in stimulating their imaginations. Help for the helper can be found in W. J. T. Mitchell's *Iconology*, which provides a background in ways of responding to imagery. The most convenient access to many of the paintings and sculptures significant for Keats is Jack's *Keats and the Mirror of Art*, which contains forty-two plates, accompanied by useful analysis and commentary.

Slides or pictures of the Elgin Marbles are among the most obvious visual aids in teaching Keats, and they are available from a variety of sources. The British Museum (London WC1B 3DG, Eng.) sells slides of them; University Prints (21 East St., PO Box 485, Winchester, MA 01890) sells a print of the entire frieze of the Parthenon in three 44-by-8-inch sheets for only a dollar. Or, slides can be made from books such as Nicholas Yalouris's *Acanthus History of Sculpture*. Whenever reproductions are made from prints in books or other sources, however, permission from the copyright holder is necessary. Slides of Wedgwood vases are frequently used in teaching "Ode on a Grecian Urn"; some are available from the Fogg Museum at Harvard University. Also valuable for this poem is Lorrain's *Landscape: The Father of Psyche Sacrificing to Apollo*, which can be found in Marcel Rothlisberger's *Claude Lorrain* or in Jack. This work can also be used to illustrate "To J. H. Reynolds, Esq." Poussin's *Kingdom of Flora* and Titian's *Bacchus and Ariadne* are used in teaching "Sleep and Poetry" (reproductions of the former are available from the Louvre and the latter from the National Gallery, Trafalgar Square, London WC2N 5DN, Eng.; both are in Jack). For "To Autumn," Poussin's *Autumn: Or, the Grapes of the Promised Land* and *Summer: Or, Ruth and Boaz*, both from the Louvre and in Jack. For "Isabella," Millais's *Isabella* and Holman Hunt's *Isabella and the Pot of Basil*, both available in *The English Dreamers*, edited by David Larkin. For *Endymion*, Wallis's *Chatterton* and Burne-Jones's *Beguiling of Merlin*, both in Larkin. For "The Eve of St. Agnes," Hunt's *Flight of Madeline and Porphyro during the Drunkenness Attending the Revelry*, in *The Pre-Raphaelites*, by the Tate, and his *Eve of St. Agnes* in Richard D. Altick's *Paintings from Books*. In Altick one can also find Daniel Maclise's *Madeline after Prayer*.

Another visual aid—the life mask of Keats—is almost guaranteed to haunt students and teachers alike. Copies in plaster can be purchased from the Keats House (Wentworth Place, Keats Grove, Hampstead, London NW3 2RR, Eng.); and photographs of it appear in all the major biographies, from Colvin to the present.

Several films, videotapes, filmstrips, and recordings pertaining to Keats are also available. Filmstrip 2 of the Films for the Humanities series *Romantic Poetry* (PO Box 2053, Princeton, NJ 08543) is a fifteen-minute sound filmstrip entitled "Byron, Shelley, and Keats." Archibald MacLeish wrote the script for the thirty-one-minute film *John Keats: Poet,* sold by the Encyclopaedia Britannica Educational Corporation; the longer version, *John Keats: His Life and Death,* lasts fifty-five minutes. Robert Gittings and Roger Sharrock have recorded a discussion of Keats and his poetry on audiocassette on the Sussex Tapes label (A28, available through Gould Media, Mt. Vernon, NY). The Annenberg-CPB Project through the University of Wisconsin Extension Service sponsored in 1987 a series of instructional tapes, with accompanying study guides, entitled *Introduction to Modern English and American Literature I: The Nineteenth Century,* which includes in program 3 the thirty-minute tape "John Keats and the Romantic Agony," by Emily Auerbach and Joseph Kestner. This tape focuses primarily on "La Belle Dame sans Merci" and "The Eve of St. Agnes" and is available only as part of the entire series, which can be ordered by calling 1-800-LEARNER. "Supplementary Tape: Readings in Romantic Poetry" contains readings of some of Keats's poetry. A number of other recordings have been made of readings of Keats's poetry as well (see bibliography of recordings).

Reading List for Students

Probably not many teachers would consider using secondary sources on Keats for freshman courses. Even sophomores have difficulty with primary materials and often allow critics' views to dominate their own, leading to some sticky issues involving intellectual honesty. Also, in courses at this level Keats is often touched on rather briefly and sometimes not until the end of the term; thus, there is usually not enough time to deal with the criticism, beyond the introduction to Keats in the text. And finally, as one questionnaire respondent observed, critical works "contribute to the pernicious notion that the object of literary study is to write an original interpretation of the works being studied." In lower-level courses secondary materials are best incorporated into lectures or class discussions in which the instructor guides students in their use.

Some would argue that even for the undergraduate Romantics course secondary materials are inappropriate unless the student is writing a paper on Keats. However, a reading list for advanced undergraduates might begin with a biography—Bush's for its brevity, Ward's more detailed work for its readability, or Bate's for its critical insights—and a brief overview (Hirst's is among the best). These can be supplemented by background readings in Chatterton, Coleridge's *Biographia Literaria,* Hazlitt's *Lectures on the En-*

glish Poets, Shakespeare, Milton, Spenser, and Wordsworth. For a single text that offers a treasure of traditional materials, Walter Jackson Bate's *Keats: A Collection of Critical Essays* in the Twentieth Century Views series contains significant and varied selections, including passages from T. S. Eliot's *Use of Poetry and the Use of Criticism*, Bush's *Mythology and the Romantic Tradition*, Fogle's *Imagery of Keats and Shelley*, Bate's *Negative Capability* and *John Keats*, Stillinger's "Hoodwinking of Madeline," Bloom's *Visionary Company*, Perkins's *Quest for Permanence*, Wasserman's *Finer Tone*, and James's *Romantic Comedy*.

Other works for a Keats reading list in a Romantics course include Lionel Trilling's "Poet As Hero: Keats in His Letters," the introduction to *Selected Letters* (rpt. in *The Opposing Self*); Douglas Bush's *Mythology and the Romantic Tradition in English Poetry*; Robert Kern's "Keats and the Problem of Romance"; Sharp's *Keats, Skepticism, and the Religion of Beauty*; Edward E. Bostetter's *Romantic Ventriloquists*; Stuart A. Ende's *Keats and the Sublime*; Stuart M. Sperry's *Keats the Poet*; Walter H. Evert's *Aesthetic and Myth in the Poetry of Keats*; G. W. Knight's *Starlit Dome*; Helen Vendler's *Odes of John Keats*; M. H. Abrams's *Mirror and the Lamp*; M. R. Ridley's *Keats' Craftsmanship*; Morris Dickstein's *Keats and His Poetry*; Charles I. Patterson's *Daemonic in the Poetry of John Keats*; Christopher Ricks's *Keats and Embarrassment*; Marilyn Butler's *Romantics, Rebels, and Reactionaries*; Leon Waldoff's *Keats and the Silent Work of Imagination*; Robert M. Ryan's *Keats: The Religious Sense*; Ian Jack's *Keats and the Mirror of Art*; Clarence Thorpe's *Mind of John Keats*; *Twentieth-Century Interpretations of Keats's Odes*, edited by Jack Stillinger; and *Twentieth-Century Interpretations of "The Eve of St. Agnes,"* edited by Alan Danzig.

Keats's Works Assigned

Keats advanced at an astonishing rate in his poetic skill from the time he took up poetry seriously. The proportion of good poems in his oeuvre, coupled with the small total number of poems, results in a fairly broad agreement concerning which of his poems ought to be taught.

"Ode to Psyche," "Ode on Melancholy," "Ode to a Nightingale," "Ode on a Grecian Urn," and "To Autumn" are the poems most frequently taught. They appear—especially "Urn," "Nightingale," and "Autumn"—in freshman introductory literature courses when no other Keats does and continue to be taught at all levels through the graduate, for reasons as varied as there are readings of these polysemous works. In a freshman class, they might be joined by "On First Looking into Chapman's Homer," whose background can be quickly and clearly supplied. The figures of speech in this poem provide textbook examples without requiring the teacher to sacrifice the sense of spontaneous discovery that the poem both expresses and contains. The brevity of all these poems makes them suitable for lower-level courses that employ close reading.

In surveys of British literature, these works are supplemented by some sonnets (frequently "When I have fears that I may cease to be," "On Seeing the Elgin Marbles," and "Bright star, would I were stedfast as thou art"), the ballad "La Belle Dame sans Merci," and the narrative "The Eve of St. Agnes" or "Lamia" or both.

Courses in the Romantic period generally attempt to capture something of Keats's growth and development as a poet. Thus, in addition to the previously mentioned works, they include "Sleep and Poetry" and "I stood tip-toe upon a little hill," which contain important statements of Keats's early poetic attitudes and ambitions. These are followed by "Dear Reynolds, as last night I lay in bed," *Endymion*, book 1 (or parts of it), and one or both of the Hyperion poems.

Keats's letters are among the best of any author. He reveals his personality and intellect with emotion, humor, candor, and spontaneity. Anyone who wants to know Keats will wish to read them all. Keats also addresses critical and aesthetic issues in his letters. As David Perkins has observed, Keats wrote of his poetic ideas and ambitions even to his brothers, neither of whom had a broad interest in poetry (*English Romantic Writers*). Keats's letters, along with his poems, ultimately make up the indispensable materials for understanding John Keats, the man and the poet. In survey courses, however, time limitations will restrict the number that can be assigned. At that level, the letters supplement an understanding and appreciation of the assigned poems and facilitate a comparison of Keats with other writers in the course. The following subject index, based on Rollins's dating and numbering and Stillinger's poem titles, will aid in selecting those letters most appropriate for the subjects and themes emphasized in individual courses.

Subject Index of Keats's Letters

"Adam's dream"—22 November 1817 (to Benjamin Bailey)
air quality, effect of—5 September 1819 (to John Taylor)
Aitken, John, invitation to Scotland—17 August 1820 (from John Aitken)
allegory—["A Man's life . . . is a continual allegory"] 19 February 1819 (to George and Georgiana Keats)

"ambitious of doing the world some good"—27 October 1818 (to Richard Woodhouse)

autumn described—21 September 1819 (to J. H. Reynolds)

Bailey, Benjamin, bad conduct with ladies—19 February 1819 (to George and Georgiana Keats)

beauty—["What the imagination seizes as Beauty must be truth"] 22 November 1817 (to Benjamin Bailey); ["snail-horn perception of Beauty"] 8 April 1818 (to B. R. Haydon); ["The mighty abstract Idea I have of Beauty"] 24 October 1818 (to George and Georgiana Keats); ["I can never feel certain of any truth but from a clear perception of its Beauty"] 31 December 1818 (to George and Georgiana Keats); ["my love of Beauty"] 8 July 1819 (to Fanny Brawne)

Brawne, Fanny, described—18 December 1818 (to George and Georgiana Keats)

Brawne, Fanny, love for—1 July 1819 (to Fanny Brawne); 8 July 1819 (to Fanny Brawne); 15 (?) July 1819 (to Fanny Brawne); 25 July 1819 (to Fanny Brawne); 5, 6 August 1819 (to Fanny Brawne); 16 August 1819 (to Fanny Brawne); 13 September 1819 (to Fanny Brawne); 11 October 1819 (to Fanny Brawne); 13 October 1819 (to Fanny Brawne); 10 (?) February 1820 (to Fanny Brawne); February (?) 1820 (to Fanny Brawne), #223; February (?) 1820 (to Fanny Brawne), #225; February (?) 1820 (to Fanny Brawne), #226; February (?) 1820 (to Fanny Brawne), #227; February (?) 1820 (to Fanny Brawne), #231; February (?) 1820 (to Fanny Brawne), #232; 24 (?) February 1820 (to Fanny Brawne); 27 (?) February 1820 (to Fanny Brawne); 28 (?) February 1820 (to Fanny Brawne); 29 (?) February 1820 (to Fanny Brawne); 1 March (?) 1820 (to Fanny Brawne); March (?) 1820 (to Fanny Brawne), #241; March (?) 1820 (to Fanny Brawne), #244; March (?) 1820 (to Fanny Brawne), #246; March (?) 1820 (to Fanny Brawne), #247; March (?) 1820 (to Fanny Brawne), #248; March (?) 1820 (to Fanny Brawne), #249; March (?) 1820 (to Fanny Brawne), #251; March (?) 1820 (to Fanny Brawne), #252; May (?) 1820 (to Fanny Brawne); June (?) 1820 (to Fanny Brawne), #262; June (?) 1820 (to Fanny Brawne), #268; 5 July (?) 1820 (to Fanny Brawne); August (?) 1820 (to Fanny Brawne); 30 September 1820 (to Charles Brown); 24 (?) October 1820 (to Mrs. Samuel Brawne); 1 November 1820 (to Charles Brown)

Brown, Charles—[story of old woman] 14, 19 February 1819 (to George and Georgiana Keats); [Keats's joke on] 25 September 1819 (to George and Georgiana Keats)

Brown, Charles Brockton, *Wieland*—21 September 1819 (to Richard Woodhouse)

Burton, Robert—[from *Anatomy of Melancholy*] 18 September 1819 (to George and Georgiana Keats)

Byron, George Gordon, Lord, compared with Keats—18 September 1819 (to George and Georgiana Keats)

"Cap and Bells, The"—see "Jealousies"

Chatterton, Thomas—["The purest English I think"] 21 September 1819 (to George and Georgiana Keats)

"cheated into some fine passages"—8 March 1819 (to B. R. Haydon)

Chesterfield, Lord—see Stanhope, Philip Dormer

Christianity—10 May 1817 (to Leigh Hunt); 14 February 1819 (to George and Georgiana Keats); 3 (?) March 1819 (to George and Georgiana Keats); 19 March 1819 (to George and Georgiana Keats); 31 March 1819 (to Fanny Keats); 21 April 1819 (to George and Georgiana Keats)

claret—19 February 1819 (to George and Georgiana Keats); 16 April 1819 (to George and Georgiana Keats)

Cobbett, William—4 March 1820 (to C. W. Dilke)

"Cockney School of Poetry"—3 November 1817 (to Benjamin Bailey)

Coleridge, Samuel Taylor, conversation with—15 April 1819 (to George and Georgiana Keats)

contemporaries most esteemed by Keats—["three things to rejoice at in this Age"] 10 January 1818 (to B. R. Haydon); ["literary kings in our Time"] 29 (?) December 1818 (to George and Georgiana Keats)

conversation—8 March 1819 (to B. R. Haydon); 10 March 1819 (from B. R. Haydon)

copyright assignment—16 September 1820 (#296: Assignment of Copyright by Keats)

"Cornwall, Barry"—see Procter, Bryan Waller

Cotterell, Miss, shipmate on Maria Crowther, shares Keats's symptoms—19 September 1820 (Joseph Severn to William Haslam)

death—["two luxuries to brood over . . . your Loveliness and the hour of my death"] 25 July 1819 (to Fanny Brawne); 14 February 1820 (to James Rice); March (?) 1820 (to Fanny Brawne), #247; March (?) 1820 (to Fanny Brawne), #252; June (?) 1820 (to Fanny Brawne), #262; August (?) 1820 (to Fanny Brawne); 16 August 1820 (to Percy Bysshe Shelley); 30 September 1820 (to Charles Brown); 1 November 1820 (to Charles Brown)

death, Keats's, described—6 March 1821 (Joseph Severn to John Taylor)

despair—["I must choose between despair & Energy—I choose the latter"] 31 May 1819 (to Sarah Jeffrey)

Dilke, Charles Wentworth, II, his opinionation—24 September 1819 (to George and Georgiana Keats)

disinterestedness—19 March 1819 (to George and Georgiana Keats)

dramatic ambition—14 August 1819 (to Benjamin Bailey); 17 November 1819 (to John Taylor)

Endymion—28 September 1817 (to B. R. Haydon); 8 October 1817 (to Benjamin Bailey); 23, 24 January 1818 (to George and Tom Keats); 27 February 1818 (to John Taylor); 9 April 1818 (to J. H. Reynolds); 24 April 1818 (to John Taylor); 27 April 1818 (to John Taylor); 8 October 1818 (to J. A. Hessey); 21 October 1818 (from Richard Woodhouse); 23 October 1818 (Richard Woodhouse to Mary Frogley); 17 December 1818 (to George and Georgiana Keats); 19 February 1819 (to George and Georgiana Keats); 18 September 1819 (to George and Georgiana Keats); 25 September 1819 (John Taylor to Richard Woodhouse); 27 July 1820 (from Percy Bysshe Shelley); 16 August 1820 (to Percy Bysshe Shelley)

"Eve of St. Agnes, The"—19 September 1819 (Richard Woodhouse to John Taylor); 22 September 1819 (to Richard Woodhouse); 25 September 1819 (John Taylor to Richard Woodhouse); 20 September 1819 (to George and Georgiana Keats); 11 (?) June 1820 (to John Taylor)

"Eve of St. Mark, The"—20 September 1819 (to George and Georgiana Keats)

experience—["Nothing ever becomes real till it is experienced"] 19 March 1819 (to George and Georgiana Keats)

fame—10 May 1817 (to Leigh Hunt); 10, 11 May 1817 (to B. R. Haydon); 9 June 1819 (to Sarah Jeffrey)

Fenbank, P.—["Sonnet to John Keats"] 29 (?) December 1818 (to George and Georgiana Keats)

"finer tone"—22 November 1817 (to Benjamin Bailey)

fine things, catalog of—1 May (?) 1819 (to Fanny Keats)

Fingal's Cave—26 July 1818 (to Tom Keats); 18 September 1819 (to George and Georgiana Keats)

foreign languages—21 September 1819 (to George and Georgiana Keats)

freedom, progress of popular—18 September 1819 (to George and Georgiana Keats)

friends, remembering—16 December 1818 (to George and Georgiana Keats)

friendship—23 January 1818 (to Benjamin Bailey); 17 March 1819 (to George and Georgiana Keats); 15 January 1820 (to Georgiana Wylie Keats)

"grand march of intellect"—3 May 1818 (to J. H. Reynolds)

Haydon, Benjamin Robert—[loan to] 12 April 1819 (from B. R. Haydon), 13 April 1819 (to B. R. Haydon); ["immortal dinner"] 5 January 1818 (to George and Tom Keats); [loan to] 20 September 1819 (to George and Georgiana Keats)

Hazlitt, William—[on *Caleb Williams*] 2 January 1819 (to George and Georgiana Keats); [on the poetry of power] [response to Gifford] 12 March 1819 (to George and Georgiana Keats); 13 March 1819 (to George and Georgiana Keats); [lectures] 10 November 1819 (to Joseph Severn), 12 November 1819 (to George and Georgiana Keats)

Keats, John, height and social class—["to be under six foot and not a lord"] 14 February 1819 (to George and Georgiana Keats)

Keats, John, illness—4 (?) February 1820 (to Fanny Brawne); 6 February 1820 (to Fanny Keats); 8 February 1820 (to Fanny Keats); 10 (?) February 1820 (to Fanny Brawne); 10 February 1820 (to Fanny Keats); February (?) 1820 (to Fanny Brawne); 14 February 1820 (to Fanny Keats); February (?) 1820 (to Fanny Brawne), #226; February (?) 1820 (to Fanny Brawne), #227; 14 February 1820 (to James Rice); 19 February 1820 (to Fanny Keats); February (?) 1820 (to Fanny Brawne), #230; February (?) 1820 (to Fanny Brawne), #231; February (?) 1820 (to Fanny Brawne), #232; 24 (?) February 1820 (to Fanny Brawne); 24 February 1820 (to Fanny Keats); 27 (?) February 1820 (to Fanny Brawne); 28 February 1820 (to J. H. Reynolds); 28 (?) February 1820 (to Fanny Brawne); 1 March (?) 1820 (to Fanny Brawne); 4 March 1820 (to C. W. Dilke); March (?) 1820 (to Fanny Brawne), #241; 8 March 1820 (Charles Brown to John Taylor); 10 March 1820 (Charles Brown to John Taylor); 13 (?) March 1820 (Charles Brown to John Taylor); March (?) 1820 (to Fanny Brawne), #246; March (?) 1820 (to Fanny Brawne), #247; March (?) 1820 (to Fanny Brawne), #248; March (?) 1820 (to Fanny Brawne), #249; 20 March 1820 (to Fanny Keats); March (?) 1820 (to Fanny Brawne), #252; 24 (?) March 1820 (to Mrs. James Wylie); 1 April 1820 (to Fanny Keats); April 1820 (to Fanny Keats); 12 April 1820 (to Fanny Keats); April (?) 1820 (to Fanny Brawne); 21 April 1820 (to Fanny Keats); 4 May 1820 (to Fanny Keats); 15 May 1820 (to Charles Brown); 18 June 1820 (from George Keats); June 1820 (from B. R. Haydon); about 21 June 1820 (to Charles Brown); 23 June 1820 (to Fanny Keats); 4 July (?) 1820 (to Fanny Brawne); 5 July 1820 (to Fanny Keats); 12 (?) July 1820 (Joseph Severn to William Haslam); 22 July 1820 (to Fanny Keats); 13 August 1820 (to John Taylor); 14 August 1820 (to Charles Brown); 16 August 1820 (to Percy Bysshe Shelley); August 1820 (to B. R. Haydon); August (?) 1820 (to B. R. Haydon); 23 August 1820 (to Fanny Keats); 23 August 1820 (to William Haslam); 11 September 1820 (to Fanny Keats); 30 September 1820 (to Charles Brown); 5 October 1820 (Charles Brown to John Taylor); 22 October 1820 (Joseph Severn to William Haslam); 24 (?) October 1820 (to Mrs. Samuel Brawne); 1 November 1820 (to Charles Brown); 1, 2 November 1820 (Joseph Severn to William Haslam); 27 November 1820 (Dr. James Clark to ?); ["I am leading a posthumous existence."] 30 November 1820 (to Charles Brown); 14, 17 December 1820 (Joseph Severn to Charles Brown); 3 January 1821 (Dr. James Clark to ?); 15 January 1821 (Joseph Severn to William Haslam); 25, 26 January 1821 (Joseph

marriage—24 October 1818 (to George and Georgiana Keats); 19 February
1819 (to George and Georgiana Keats); 17 September 1819 (to George
and Georgiana Keats); 8 November 1820 (from George Keats)

Massinger, Philip—[from *Duke of Milan*] 1 July 1819 (to Fanny Brawne)

medicine, practicing—3 (?) March 1819 (to George and Georgiana Keats);
26 May 1819 (to Fanny Keats); 31 May 1819 (to Sarah Jeffrey); June
1819 (to C. W. Dilke); 9 June 1819 (to Sarah Jeffrey); 9 June 1819 (to
Fanny Keats); 22 September 1819 (to Charles Brown)

Milton, John—[from *Comus*] 24 March 1818 (to James Rice); 19 March 1819
(to George and Georgiana Keats); ["Life to him would be death to
me."] 21 September 1819 (to George and Georgiana Keats); [*Paradise
Lost*] 21 September 1819 (to George and Georgiana Keats)

nature, beauty of—14 February 1820 (to James Rice)

"Negative Capability"—21, 27 (?) December 1817 (to George and Tom Keats)

"Ode to a Nightingale"—15 January 1820 (to Georgiana Wylie Keats)

Otho the Great—28 August 1819 (to Fanny Keats); 5 September 1819 (to
John Taylor); 17 September 1819 (to George and Georgiana Keats); 12
November 1819 (to George and Georgiana Keats); December 1819 (to
James Rice); 20 December 1819 (to Fanny Keats); 13 January 1820 (to
Georgiana Wylie Keats)

pains of existence—["Man is originally 'a poor forked creature' "] 21 April
1819 (to George and Georgiana Keats); ["I have never known any
unalloy'd Happiness"] 1 July 1819 (to Fanny Brawne); 13 September
1819 (to Fanny Brawne); 23 September 1819 (to Charles Brown)

parsons, Keats's hatred of—14 February 1819 (to George and Georgiana
Keats); 3 (?) March 1819 (to George and Georgiana Keats)

"passive and receptive"—19 February 1818 (to J. H. Reynolds)

perfectibility—21 April 1819 (to George and Georgiana Keats)

"Peter Bell," review of—21 April 1819 (to George and Georgiana Keats)

Philips, Katherine Fowler (Mrs. James)—[from "To Mrs. M. A. at Parting"]
21 September 1817 (to J. H. Reynolds)

philosophy—["poetry . . . not so fine a thing as philosophy"] 19 March 1819
(to George and Georgiana Keats); 21 April 1819 (to George and Georgiana Keats); ["I hope I am a little more of a Philosopher . . . less of
a versifying Pet-lamb"] 9 June 1819 (to Sarah Jeffrey); February (?)
1820 (to Fanny Brawne), #231; 24 (?) February 1820 (to Fanny Brawne);
30 November 1820 (to Charles Brown)

"Pleasure Thermometer"—30 January 1818 (to John Taylor)

poems by Keats included in letters—["To George Felton Mathew"] November 1815 (to G. F. Mathew); ["To My Brother George"] August 1816
(to George Keats); ["To Charles Cowden Clarke"] September 1816 (to
C. C. Clarke); ["Addressed to the Same"] 20 November 1816 (to B. R.

Haydon); ["Addressed to the Same"] 21 November 1816 (to B. R. Haydon); ["On the Sea"] 17 April 1817 (to J. H. Reynolds); ["The Gothic looks solemn"] September 1817 (to J. H. Reynolds); [from *Endymion*] 28 October 1817 (to Benjamin Bailey); [from *Endymion*] 31 October 1817 (to Jane Reynolds); [from *Endymion*] 3 November 1817 (to Benjamin Bailey); [from *Endymion*] 22 November 1817 (to J. H. Reynolds); ["Lines on Seeing a Lock of Milton's Hair"] 23 January 1818 (to Benjamin Bailey); ["On Sitting Down to Read *King Lear* Once Again"] 23 January 1818 (to George and Tom Keats); [from *Endymion*] 30 January 1818 (to John Taylor); ["O blush not so! O blush not so"] 31 January 1818 (to J. H. Reynolds); ["Hence burgundy, claret, and port"] 31 January 1818 (to J. H. Reynolds); ["God of the meridian"] 31 January 1818 (to J. H. Reynolds); ["When I have fears that I may cease to be"] 31 January 1818 (to J. H. Reynolds); ["O thou whose face hath felt the winter's wind"] 19 February 1818 (to J. H. Reynolds); ["Four seasons fill the measure of the year"] 13 March 1818 (to Benjamin Bailey); ["For there's Bishop's Teign"] 21 March 1818 (to B. R. Haydon); ["Over the hill and over the dale"] 24 March 1818 (to James Rice); ["Dear Reynolds, as last night I lay in bed"] 25 March 1818 (to J. H. Reynolds); ["Mother of Hermes! and still youthful Maia"] 3 May 1818 (to J. H. Reynolds); ["Give me your patience, sister, while I frame"] 27 June 1818 (to George and Georgiana Keats); ["Sweet, sweet is the greeting of eyes"] 28 June 1818 (to George and Georgiana Keats); ["On Visiting the Tomb of Burns"] 1 July 1818 (to Tom Keats); ["Old Meg she was a gipsey"] 2 July 1818 (to Fanny Keats); ["There was a naughty boy"] 3 July 1818 (to Fanny Keats); ["Old Meg she was a gipsey"] 3 July 1818 (to Tom Keats); ["Ah! ken ye what I met the day"] 10 July 1818 (to Tom Keats); ["To Ailsa Rock"] 10 July 1818 (to Tom Keats); ["All gentle folks who owe a grudge"] 17 July 1818 (to Tom Keats); ["Of late two dainties were before me plac'd"] 18 July 1818 (to Tom Keats); ["There is a joy in footing slow across a silent plain"] 22 July 1818 (to Benjamin Bailey); ["Not Aladdin magian"] 26 July 1818 (to Tom Keats); ["Upon my life, Sir Nevis, I am piqu'd"] 3 August 1818 (to Tom Keats); ["Read me a lesson, Muse, and speak it loud"] 6 August 1818 (to Tom Keats); ["'Tis the 'witching time of night' "] 14 October 1818 (to George and Georgiana Keats); ["Fancy"] 2 January 1819 (to George and Georgiana Keats); ["Bards of passion and of mirth"] 2 January 1819 (to George and Georgiana Keats); ["I had a dove, and the sweet dove died"] 3 January 1819 (to George and Georgiana Keats); ["Why did I laugh tonight? No voice will tell"] 19 March 1819 (to George and Georgiana Keats); ["When they were come unto the Faery's court"] 15 April 1819 (to George and Georgiana Keats); ["Character of C. B."] 16 April 1819 (to George and Georgiana Keats); ["As Hermes once took to his feathers light"] 16 April 1819 (to George and Georgiana Keats); ["La Belle Dame sans Merci"] 21 April 1819 (to George and Georgiana Keats); ["Song of Four Fairies"] 21 April 1819 (to George and Georgiana Keats); ["On Fame" ("How fever'd is the man")] 21 April 1819 (to George and Georgiana Keats); ["On Fame" ("Fame, like a wayward girl")] 30 April 1819 (to George and Georgiana Keats); ["To Sleep"] 30 April 1819 (to George and Georgiana Keats); ["Ode to Psyche"] 30 April 1819 (to George and Georgiana Keats); ["Two or three posies"] 1 May (?) 1819 (to Fanny Keats); ["If by dull rhymes our English must be chain'd"] 3 May 1819 (to George and Georgiana Keats); [from "Lamia"] 5 September 1819 (to John Taylor); ["Pensive they sit, and roll their languid eyes"] 17 September 1819 (to George and Georgiana Keats); ["Give me your patience, sister, while I frame"] 18 September 1819 (to George and Georgiana Keats); ["Not Aladdin magian"] 18 September 1819 (to George and Georgiana Keats); ["The Eve of St. Mark"] 20 September 1819 (to George and Georgiana Keats); ["—Als writith he of swevenis"] 20 September 1819 (to George and Georgiana Keats); ["To Autumn"; from "The Fall of Hyperion"] 21 September 1819 (to Richard Woodhouse); ["La platonique chevalresque"] 21 September 1819 (to Richard Woodhouse); [from "The Fall of Hyperion"] 21 September 1819 (to Richard Woodhouse); [from *Otho the Great*] 27 September 1819 (to George and Georgiana Keats)

"poetical Character, the"—27 October 1818 (to Richard Woodhouse); about 27 October 1818 (Richard Woodhouse to John Taylor)

poetic "Axioms"—27 February 1818 (to John Taylor)

"Poetry should be great & unobtrusive"—3 February 1818 (to J. H. Reynolds)

politics—["inclined to the liberal side of things"] 22 December 1818 (to George and Georgiana Keats); 18 September 1819 (to George and Georgiana Keats); ["I will write, on the liberal side of the question. . . ."] 22 September 1819 (to Charles Brown); 22 September 1819 (to C. W. Dilke)

Procter, Bryan Waller—28 February 1820 (to J. H. Reynolds); 4 March 1820 (to C. W. Dilke)

"Public, the"—9 April 1818 (to J. H. Reynolds)

quarantine in Italy—22 October 1820 (Joseph Severn to William Haslam); 24 (?) October 1820 (to Mrs. Samuel Brawne)

reading—17, 18 April 1817 (to J. H. Reynolds); 19 February 1818 (to J. H. Reynolds); 3 October 1819 (with Charles Brown to B. R. Haydon)

"real" and "semireal"—13 March 1818 (to Benjamin Bailey); *see* "experience"

real/imaginary woes—17 September 1819 (to George and Georgiana Keats); 23 September 1819 (to Charles Brown)

women in Keats's writing—["there is a tendency to class women in my books with roses and sweetmeats"] August (?) 1820 (to Charles Brown)

Woodhouse, Richard, Jr., offer of loan—16 September 1820 (from Richard Woodhouse)

Wordsworth, William—[from "Ode: Intimations of Immortality"] 31 May 1819 (to Sarah Jeffrey)

writing compared with speaking—20 September 1819 (to George and Georgiana Keats)

Papers and Other Assignments

For sophomore British literature survey courses, journals can be useful, and there are several kinds of exercises that might be done. In large part, the value of a journal is to encourage the students to become engaged with what they read and to record their responses. The responses need not wait until the entire poem has been read. For instance, one teacher reports asking students to pause at a given line and try to predict what the author will do in the rest of the work. At other times, the teacher asks students to write about a specific character, idea, or passage; to create a dialogue between themselves and one of the characters in the poem or between two characters in different works; to compare the work being read with some other literary work; or to develop some aspect of the work in a creative piece, using the work as a model. Other teachers have students copy down their favorite passages. One teacher has students leave blank pages opposite each journal entry to allow her to enter into a dialogue with them or to allow the students to respond to something previously written. That dialogue can become more public, too, if the student reads a passage from the journal in class to start a discussion.

For more formal writing assignments at the sophomore level, most teachers find it productive to restrict their assignments to primary materials, since many students have not achieved the sophistication necessary to handle secondary materials directly without either misunderstanding or being overwhelmed by them. Here are assignments some teachers use:

1.

A number of Romantic poems are about dejection, loss, or alienation. Choose two of the following works, and explain the problem or sorrow each one laments (its nature, source, and consequences), the speaker's reaction to the problem and the degree to which a solution is achieved, and the particular images or other poetic techniques used to convey the mood or dilemma. Compare and contrast.

> Wordsworth, "Tintern Abbey" or *The Prelude*, book 1
> Coleridge, "Dejection: An Ode"
> Shelley, "Hymn to Intellectual Beauty" or "Ode to the West Wind"
> Keats, "La Belle Dame sans Merci"
> Byron, *Manfred*
>
> (Beth Lau, Ripon College)

2.

Many Romantic poems you have read wrestle with a conflict between opposing impulses or states of being, which can be expressed in a number of different ways: innocence and experience, ideal and real, mortality and immortality, faith and doubt, aspiration and resignation, and so on. Choose a poem by Keats and characterize precisely the opposing forces, tendencies, or conditions that are in conflict. Which side of the conflict wins in the end?

> (Beth Lau, Ripon College)

3.

The beauty and intellectual substance of Keats's letters are almost as famous as his poetry. Select one passage from a Keats letter that deals with literature or literary subjects, and write a detailed analysis of it in relation to one of his poems on the reading list. You should pay close attention to matters of style and imagery as well as to theme or argument.

> (Nicholas O. Warner, Claremont McKenna College)

4.

One critic has said that the chief strength of Keats's poetry is his ability to "give complete and powerful expression to the human longing for a better world" and at the same time to "remain faithful to the critical intelligence that forces us to acknowledge that dreams are only dreams and that in the sole world we know values are tragically in conflict" (Perkins, *English Romantic Writers* 1117–18). He says, "the course of Keats's greatest poems reflects this insight."

Show that this statement is true by applying it specifically to at least three of Keats's poems (more if possible). Then choose the poem that best fits this description or achieves the quality stated, and explain your choice. If you think another poem—one that does not fit the critic's description—is *the* greatest one, say why briefly.

(Ruth L. Wright, Auburn University)

5.

Is there a logic in the progress of Keats's Great Odes from "Psyche" to "Autumn"? What is the logical progression of the odes? Include all the odes in dealing with this problem.

(Mario L. D'Avanzo, Queens College)

For upper-level Romantics courses, papers often involve secondary sources. A bibliographical essay on one of Keats's poems might be assigned, since the scholarship on Keats is rich and varied. An assignment asking students to incorporate scholarship and criticism into their own interpretations of Keats's writing should provide guidance in handling the material. The following assignment will illustrate:

Your culminating paper in this class provides an opportunity for you to read and think further about a poem you have already written about (in journal entries and, possibly, short papers growing out of them). To deepen your knowledge of that poem and to develop your critical sensibilities, read four articles or excerpts from books pertaining to the poem. The criticism will vary widely in approach: some will be clear and illuminating, some turgid, some—well, you decide. Read the articles closely before you attempt to write anything.

Your paper should be a well-organized, carefully written response to the following matters:

1. What are the major and minor points of each article or excerpt?
2. What assumptions do you think the critics bring to their scholarship?
3. How well do the writers make their points? Use examples to support your assertions.
4. How do the four critics' readings of the poem agree and differ with one another? Note the points of agreement and difference, and, if possible, explain why.
5. Compare your initial reading of the poem with your final reading, a response informed by your having studied these critics' views. What remains the same in your reading and why? What has changed and why?

(Mary A. Quinn, University of San Diego)

Although journals are not commonly used in upper-level Romantics courses, when they are used students can benefit by consulting secondary sources. Some teachers require students to read Keats criticism for three hours a week and to summarize that reading and comment on it in a journal. Other teachers stipulate that journal entries should be evenly divided between primary and secondary materials.

Even when writing assignments do not require the student to deal with the criticism, they are more complex and sophisticated than those in survey courses of British literature. Here is an example:

> Despite the diversity of poetic forms he employs and the variety of subjects, styles, and themes he essays, Keats's poetry can be seen to proceed cumulatively. There are doublings-back, of course, wrong tracks taken, failures both notable and forgettable, but through this short career one still gets the sense of forward movement, of aspiration single-mindedly pursued. One thing that clearly contributes to this sense is the extent to which Keats steals (as it were) from himself. It is obvious that he admired and used materials from other poets— Shakespeare, Spenser, Milton, Wordsworth, to name but the major ones; perhaps less obvious is the way he used his already written poems in the writing of later poems. He repeats lines, words, phrases, images, metaphors, even characters and scenes—but even as he reuses them he usually transforms them, retextualizes them, to accord with the thematic (or other) exigencies of the poem he is creating.
>
> Your assignment, then, is to choose one of the odes ("Psyche," "Indolence," "Melancholy," "Nightingale," "Urn," or "Autumn") and, with the help of an imaginatively used concordance, seek out in the earlier poems those materials (and language) out of which (in part, of course) Keats creates the ode you're dealing with. What is the nature of the borrowing? How is the borrowing changed or modified? To what uses is it put in the ode? When we recognize the borrowing, how does it affect our reading and interpretation of the ode? Does our knowledge of the earlier poems help us to interpret the ode? Does the borrowing indicate that the ode is working out a problem similar to that in the earlier poem? What does that tell us about the nature of the problem—and its at least potential resolution?
>
> Remember: this is not a paper in which you are being asked to compare the ode with another poem or poems. Your focus is on one ode and the various uses to which Keats puts materials borrowed from himself. Some of those uses, of course, may not involve a transformation of their original import; in such cases you should try to determine why that is so, what effect it has on the borrowing's new contextualization.

But you should be especially attentive to the ways in which the borrowed material is transformed in the transaction, the probable reasons (as you see them) for the transformation, and the effect of the transformed borrowing on your interpretation of the ode.

(Robert F. Gleckner, Duke University)

To supplement their lectures and to prompt students' journal entries, some teachers distribute study questions to help students identify particular issues. Consider the following heuristic for "Lamia":

> Critics have divided between calling "Lamia" Keats's most perfect poem (at least in the narrative vein) and his most unpleasant poem. Keats himself thought "there is that sort of fire in it which must take hold of people in some way—give them either pleasant or unpleasant sensation" (*Letters* 2: 189). Besides this, it is probably Keats's most enigmatic poem: What did he mean by it? Which side was he on— Lamia's, Lycius's, or Apollonius's? And how can one decide?
>
> By way of preface, reread "The Eve of St. Mark" and "La Belle Dame sans Merci"—the last especially is almost a preview of "Lamia." To what extent can we see Keats's changing relationship to Fanny Brawne reflected in all three of these poems? What recurrent images do you find? Keats is turning to a new model of style in "Lamia," that of Dryden—as demonstrated, for instance, in his translations of Ovid and Chaucer. What are the special features of this new style in "Lamia"? Is it better adapted for storytelling than, say, the Spenserian stanzas of "The Eve of St. Agnes"?
>
> Narrative structure: What is the point of prefacing the story of Lamia and Lycius with the long account of Hermes and his nymph? In many ways "Lamia" has a dramatic structure. Can the poem be described in terms of scenes, dialogue, setting, and the general shape of a tragic plot—tragic conflict, foreshadowing, suspense, climax, ironic reversal, and tragic recognition?
>
> Characters: What values does each character represent? What, especially, is the character of Lamia—woman or serpent?
>
> Relation to source (the tale from Burton's *Anatomy of Melancholy*): What does Keats add to Burton? What does he actually change?
>
> Themes: "Lamia" brings together a number of Keats's central preoccupations—the nature and value of dreams, the conflict between (or possible reconciliation of) sensation and thought, the meaning of sexual love. Which do you think is the central theme here? Does Keats's attitude toward it seem to be taking a new direction in "Lamia"?

(Aileen Ward, New York University)

Testing is so much a function of the way a course is taught that to prescribe or even describe how a knowledge of Keats should be tested is problematical. Most teachers favor a combination of factual and essay questions. The factual questions may require short answers or the identification and brief discussion of passages. In survey courses, essays often ask students to compare Keats with other writers in the course or to demonstrate his relation to some aspect of Romanticism. In upper-level Romanticism courses, students are frequently asked to come to terms with the broad sweep of Keats's career or to assess an aspect of his contribution to Romanticism. Often, teachers press students to define in their essays what is "distinctively Keatsian."

Part Two

APPROACHES

INTRODUCTION

Although the essays that follow are gathered into three groups, categorized roughly as classroom strategies, theoretical approaches, and thematic orientations, virtually all have implications for one or both of the other categories. At the extremes, individual essays perhaps address different audiences, persons at different levels of experience or of involvement with Romantic studies. Yet we believe that each represents the solution to someone's problem or the enhancement of someone's interest, and that there is something in each of value to all.

While this series tries to accommodate both traditional and innovative orientations, its aim is not to prescribe what or how anyone should teach but rather to present a balanced spectrum of the ways that collectively we do teach. One implication of the responses we received is that the revolution of theory has become a de facto revolution of praxis as well. The productive arc of Keats's brief career once seemed to require at least a glance at the pre-*Endymion* poetry, in search of intellectual bloodlines and foreshadowings of the annus mirabilis to come. Our contemporary view, however, which sees poets as more shaped by, than shapers of, the collective values of their times, tends to preclude that kind of inquiry. Instead of ratifying the self-privileging Romantic mystique of individual creative genius, we emphasize the writing as a surrogate for the writer. Keats's thought processes, conscious and unconscious, remain matters of interest, but, as often as not, we seek evidence in the writing of ambiguities, assumptions, evasions, and suppressions at the margins of consciousness, or below it altogether.

Another shift from former teaching emphases is the absence of extended commentary on the sonnets. Some contributors mention one or another of them as indicative of a Keatsian turn or moment, but no one proposed a free-standing, contextualized discussion of how to deal in the classroom with a unique poetic kind that works, in the hands of each poet, both within and against its own history—and that was a sort of touchstone challenge to Keats throughout his writing career. Perhaps the feeling is that the handling of a particular form is irrelevant to contemporary interest, unless the subject fits into a context of ongoing concern—in which case its "sonnetness" is irrelevant.

The first group of essays, "Classroom Strategies," attempts to help students interact with the poems, the better to help them see. None of the approaches tells them what they must see; all jar them out of easy answers and complacency. Leon Waldoff identifies an apparent crux or point of ambiguity in "The Eve of St. Agnes" and sets students to finding evidence within the poem for one or another of the interpretive alternatives. John E. Grant, using "La Belle Dame sans Merci," argues for a teaching approach that avoids leading students into premature interpretive commitment and emphasizes the mature acceptance of multiple interpretive possibilities. Frank Jordan describes a method of teaching the odes in which teams of students become "experts" on each of the odes and take turns in presenting the poems' possibilities and meeting the class's challenges; and Brian Wilkie tells about requiring student debates in which the many viewpoints enforced by the debate format discourage a simplistic reading of the poems in favor of a more problematic complexity. Applying his diagrammatic technique to the "Grecian Urn" and "Nightingale" odes, Bruce Clarke illustrates everything from the simplest relations of denotation and connotation to the increasingly complex dynamics of whole poems. Finally, Lore Metzger presents the "Nightingale" ode first in the traditional formalist mode, then invites an ironic reading more interinvolved with the world outside the poem's immediate experience.

In the next section, "Theoretical Approaches," it may seem odd, in an era of predominantly theoretical interest, that so few of the essays address themselves programmatically to the application of theory in the classroom. The explanation lies partly in our wishing to maintain a balance of kinds within the volume and partly (given a rationale of reflecting, rather than dictating, norms) in our having to work within the limits of what was offered. What struck us most forcibly throughout, however, was the extent to which theoretical emphases were subsumed in essays that had other orientations. For example, although we were not offered a comprehensive Marxist critique, Louise Z. Smith's essay on composition theory in the literary classroom glances at a Marxist reading of "Isabella" almost as an interpretation to be taken for granted; and it would be hard not to see a shadow of things to come in Metzger's bifocal reading of the "Nightingale" ode. Again, while Susan Wolfson offers a comprehensive critique of Keats's poetry from a feminist perspective, Nancy Moore Goslee through literary history and Donald C. Goellnicht through reader-response theory arrive at conclusions compatible with Wolfson's—in effect verifying answers to questions that less theoretically focused generations never thought to ask. Although psychoanalytic criticism lacked the staying power to survive in a theoretical essay, the spirit of psychoanalytic reading is evident in the contributions of Jean Hall, Peter J. Manning, and Susan Wolfson. Yet again, Manning and Metzger reflect the mindset of Tilottama Rajan's more systematically argued deconstructive phenomenology. The point of these comparisons is that, while five theoretical essays limit themselves to single-focus teaching perspectives (Rajan's deconstructive phenomenology, Wolfson's feminism, Nicholas Warner's interart analogies, Smith's composition theory, and Goellnicht's reader-response), these perspectives are not arid abstractions but definitions and demonstrations of points of view that work and, as the evidence of the other essays shows, have already been varyingly assimilated to the classroom by the profession at large.

Among the essays in "Thematic Orientations," the third group, Wolf Z. Hirst's analyses of *Endymion*, the "Ode to Psyche," and the Hyperion poems show how knowledge of the myths on which Keats based some of his most important poems can be used to explore his several positions on the fantasy-reality spectrum. Goslee's approach to *Endymion* through prototypical figures in the older literatures of Keats's acquaintance sheds light on our reading of such later works as "La Belle Dame," "The Eve of St. Agnes," and "Lamia." Ronald A. Sharp, reminding us of the many ways that death impinged on Keats's consciousness and drawing on modern research in the psychology of death and dying, demonstrates how that awareness can be used to identify a major substratum in the odes and elsewhere. Jean Hall orients her teaching around the problem of imagination as she thinks Keats perceived it—essentially preemptive in the romances but safely redirected in the reflexivity of the odes. And finally, Manning proposes an approach to the "Ode on a Grecian Urn" that reproduces in our experience of reading the poem the experience of the poet as he reads the urn. Beyond that, the essay raises profound questions about the practical limits of interacting with art in any form or of entering wholly into any experience not our own.

If there is any single characteristic that mediates the diversity of these essays, it is clearly the abhorrence of interpretive closure in teaching. While that is perhaps the benchmark of our moment, one would like to believe that it is always a component of the active mind, in and out of the classroom. In any case, these essays are presented not as containments of possibility but as incitements of the kind that Keats called "starting post[s] towards all 'the two-and thirty Pallaces.' " We hope they'll help you on your way.

NOTE: All quotations from Keats's poetry in this volume are from Jack Stillinger's Belknap-Harvard edition of 1978, and all quotations of letters are from Hyder Edward Rollins's edition.

CLASSROOM STRATEGIES

The Question of Porphyro's Stratagem

Leon Waldoff

Some adaptation of the Socratic method to the nature of a subject and the demands of a course is no doubt a feature of all effective teaching. Most common, perhaps, is the use of questions to initiate a discussion. The critics who teach us the most are typically, like Lionel Trilling, masters of the art of posing central questions and defining crucial issues. When teaching Keats I begin with a question about the action, the development of thought, the characterization, the tone, or another important aspect of the work. My purpose is to involve the students as fully as possible in the process of interpretation—examining certain passages at length, drawing appropriate inferences, and constructing a coherent understanding of the poem. Ideally, the question centers on an uncertainty in the text that proves a crux of interpretation and that points to a prominent theme or to a major preoc- cupation of the poet. Identifying such an uncertainty is intended to activate a process of discovery, generating insight, clarifying the moral, psychological, philosophical, or other content of the work, and revealing important features of Keats's poetry. Several of Keats's poems lend themselves well to this approach, but none better than "The Eve of St. Agnes."

At the heart of the poem lies the question of whether Porphyro's stratagem, mentioned in stanza 16 but never described, includes the sexual consum- mation that takes place in stanza 36. Was the "thought" that "came like a full-blown rose, / Flushing his brow" (136–37) a plan of seduction? Students instinctively recognize the question as important and often seize on some sexual, psychological, or moral issue raised by it. (A few years ago a student, a woman of fifty and mother of three, banged her fist on her desk while insisting that Porphyro was a sneak and should be arrested!) What they do not so readily see are the complications of evidence, inference, and interpretation in which a reader necessarily becomes involved in attempting to determine what Porphyro's stratagem includes and why it is important to an understanding of the poem. More specifically, they tend not to see that Madeline's observance of the rituals connected with St. Agnes' Eve, her dream, and Porphyro's stratagem are all part of a complex attitude that the poem represents toward imagination. Of the three, the stratagem is the one we know the least about and the one most open to critical controversy.

Before introducing the question of Porphyro's stratagem, however, I try to ensure a firmer grasp of the action, the dialogue, and the narrator's commentary by playing Ralph Richardson's reading of the poem. It takes twenty-five minutes and, aside from alerting students to special features of Keats's language (for example, the pronunciation of unmarked but accented endings of participial adjectives in combinations such as "wreathed pearls" and "warmed jewels" [227, 228]), it greatly intensifies their response to the poem. Though Richardson's reading is not perfect, he does bring the voices of Angela, Porphyro, and Madeline to life, enabling one to hear their surprise or passion or disappointment. He is especially effective in dramatizing Angela's shock and busy fear on first seeing Porphyro in the castle ("Mercy, Porphyro! hie thee from this place. . . . Get Hence! get hence!" [98–100]) and in conveying a sense of the narrator's excited identification with Porphyro ("Now prepare, / Young Porphyro, for gazing on that bed; / She comes, she comes again, like ring-dove fray'd and fled" [196–98]).

Immediately after Richardson's reading I ask a series of warm-up questions: What is the legend on which the poem is based? Who is the beadsman and what is he doing? Who is the first person Porphyro encounters in the castle? What does Angela say to him? Some editions of Keats's poetry and some anthologies provide answers to the first two questions in footnotes or endnotes, but the purpose of the questions is not to test the students. It is rather to concentrate their attention on the actions, events, and statements and to reconstruct through discussion the progress of the narrative through stanza 36, when, invariably, some students hesitantly reveal that they do not understand that a sexual consummation is supposed to take place. These students enact a version of Madeline's surprise and themselves question Porphyro's intentions.

At this point in the discussion I divide the question into two parts, loading each with a share of the critical implications that need to be examined. Has Porphyro all along intended to seduce Madeline? If so, he appears a person less than heroic and the poem an expression of a skeptical, ironic, and antiromantic view of dreams, dreamers, and imagination. Or has he sought only to awaken her in the midst of her dreaming in order to ensure, according to the legend, that he will be her future husband? If this is his intention, he seems to make Madeline's dream come true (though in ways she has not expected), and the poem affirms romance and the power of imagination to bring desire to fulfillment. Though oversimplified, these are the two principal views of this question in the criticism. In the former, the imagination, represented by Madeline's dream, is self-deceiving and seductive; in the latter, the imagination, represented by Porphyro's stratagem and the poem's strong though never unqualified commitment to romance, is wish-fulfilling and adaptive. Posing the question of the stratagem in this way, and incorporating into it the larger question of the definition and role of imagination in the poem, builds a bridge for students between different levels of understanding—on the one hand, the more literal level of specific actions, events, statements, and on the other, the interpretive level of inference, significance, generalization.

Identifying and evaluating the evidence in support of one view or the other now becomes the liveliest part of the discussion, and students naturally and independently turn to much of the same evidence that critics have used. Angela's shock when Porphyro proposes his stratagem ("A cruel man and impious thou art" [140]), Porphyro's willingness to hide in a closet and watch Madeline undress, the narrator's comment that she is "Hoodwink'd with faery fancy" (70), the sexually suggestive metaphors used to characterize Porphyro's feelings ("purple riot," "burning," "throbbing star" [138, 159, 318]), the comparison of Porphyro with Merlin, Madeline's disappointment when awakened, and her claim after the sexual consummation that Porphyro is "Cruel" (330) and that she is "a deceived thing" (332)—all are pointed to by students who argue that Porphyro intended to seduce Madeline. Other students, usually about half the class, argue that the legend rather than seduction is the key to the stratagem (particularly Porphyro's appearing to Madeline in the midst of her dream to represent himself as her future husband) and cite as evidence that Porphyro, despite Angela's initial reaction to him, swears his devotion to Madeline and win's Angela's help ("Good Angela, believe me by these tears" [150]); that he tries to awaken Madeline and is himself half asleep in the lap of legends of old ("So mus'd awhile, entoil'd in woofed phantasies" [288]); that he invokes the terms of old romance, calling himself Madeline's "vassal blest" and "beauty's shield" (335, 336); that she invites him to stay; that he calls her his bride; and that, instead of having planned seduction, he is only carried away by his passion, Madeline's "voluptuous accents" (317), and the enchantment of St. Agnes' Eve.

Students on both sides of the argument usually mention such additional evidence as the narrator's description of Porphyro's aim in coming to the castle:

> [he] implores
> All saints to give him sight of Madeline,
> But for one moment in the tedious hours,
> That he might gaze and worship all unseen;
> Perchance speak, kneel, touch, kiss—in sooth such things have been
>   (77–81);

the depiction of Porphyro's "wish":

> Which was, to lead him, in close secrecy,
> Even to Madeline's chamber, and there hide
> Him in a closet, of such privacy
> That he might see her beauty unespied,
> And win perhaps that night a peerless bride
>   (163–67);

and Angela's insistence that he must marry Madeline:

> Ah! thou must needs the lady wed,
> Or may I never leave my grave among the dead"
>   (179–80).

They are also quick to see the relevance of Keats's letter to Benjamin Bailey on 22 November 1817, with its confidence in the power of imagination and its highly problematic analogy to Madeline's dream: "What the imagination seizes as Beauty must be truth—whether it existed before or not. . . . The Imagination may be compared to Adam's dream—he awoke and found it truth" (*Letters* 1: 184–85).

After the implications in these and other passages have been explored at some length (the apparent progression in "speak, kneel, touch, kiss" [81] and the problematic analogy between Madeline's dream and Adam's usually draw the most commentary) and the students' views of the poem clearly outlined, I distribute copies of the section of the letter to Taylor in which Woodhouse reports Keats's remark that he "sh[oul]d despise a man who would be such an eunuch in sentiment as to leave a maid, with that Character about her, in such a situation: & sho[ul]d despise himself to write about it" (*Letters* 2: 163). I ask the students if this remark offers any clues to Keats's conception of Porphyro's intentions. Did Keats believe the sexual consummation was part of the plan of seduction or rather the result of the power of spontaneous action "in such a situation"? However the students answer, I refer them to the rejected revision of lines 314–22, to which Keats's publisher, John Taylor, registered a strong objection and in which Keats is more explicit about the crucial moment ("his arms encroaching slow, / Have zoned her, heart to heart. . . . his quick rejoinder flows / Into her burning ear").

At the end of the discussion I do not present an "accepted" or "correct" interpretation. On the contrary, I emphasize that the two (or more) opinions of Porphyro's stratagem and of the poem's attitude toward imagination reflect the diversity in the criticism over the last twenty-five years and help to define the larger problem of imagination in Keats's poetry and thought. I urge the students to determine for themselves when we read the other great poems of 1819—particularly "La Belle Dame sans Merci," "Ode to Psyche," "Ode to a Nightingale," "Ode on a Grecian Urn," and "Lamia"—what Keats's attitude toward imagination is and how it can be related to other views of this celebrated Romantic concept, especially those of Wordsworth, Coleridge, and Shelley. Among the paper topics for the course, I often include one on "The Eve of St. Agnes" that asks students to reconsider the issues raised in the class, to read Jack Stillinger ("Hoodwinking") and Stuart Sperry ("Romance")—the two most influential critics of the poem—and to write an essay setting forth and defending their own views. In undergraduate honors or graduate seminars, I provide a more comprehensive list of critics to read.

No single approach can fully illuminate a poem, of course, and there is much else in "The Eve of St. Agnes" that needs to be discussed: Keats's use of the Spenserian stanza, the sensuousness of his imagery, the blend of fairy tale and Gothic romance, the complex tone of the narrator, and the uncertainties of the ending. But in the two or three class hours usually devoted to "The Eve of St. Agnes," there is time to say only a few words about these special features. My approach through a problem of interpretation, however, has several advantages. More often than not, the discussion of this poem is the liveliest of the semester. Some students experience frustration when they see that much of the evidence can be used, with only a slight change of emphasis, to support a different viewpoint, and they are disappointed when I tell them that there is no definitive interpretation of the poem. But most are excited by the challenge of arguing for one interpretation or another or of working out a third that mediates between the two principal ones. In addition, many distinctive qualities of Keats's poetic art—the use of the romance mode, the medieval setting, the dramatic character of the narrative, the richness of the imagery, the preoccupation with imagination, the presence of an ironic perspective—achieve a stronger hold in the students' memories because the poem is discussed in a well-defined critical context.

Most important is the transfer from teacher to student of the responsibility for developing and defending an interpretation. Rather than something given by the teacher or, worse, arbitrarily imposed on the poem, interpretation is represented for what it is: an argument gathering together the many different and sometimes conflicting strands of a work into a coherent view. By focusing on a crucial uncertainty in a poem, and on the evidence relating to it, students learn to construct such an argument. And in this way the uncertainty that initiates a classroom discussion becomes an introduction not only to some of the main issues of Keats criticism but to the nature of critical dialogue.

Discovering "La Belle Dame sans Merci"

John E. Grant

The charm, brevity, and accessibility of "La Belle Dame sans Merci" have encouraged teachers to include it in many courses where Romanticism is not considered an issue. Simply as a famous lyrical ballad, it has a strong claim to the student's attention. This poem can prove more discussable for general education students than any of Keats's Great Odes can simply because the words are deployed tersely, in the ballad manner, rather than in Keats's luxuriant mode. Though it may seem extravagant to schedule two class meetings for consideration of so brief a poem, "La Belle Dame sans Merci" appears to best advantage when it is first discussed and then reconsidered after an interval. The longer a teacher can delay the imposition of an interpretation —resisting the apodictic pressure of most textbook presentations—the better the poem will serve the purposes of education.

For an effective opening move, the teacher might distribute a few days in advance of discussion unannotated texts of both versions of the poem, without mentioning the fact that most critics have preferred the 1819 version (the Brown transcript: see *Poems*, ed. Stillinger, 1978) to the 1820 version published in the *Indicator*. As students, undirected, consider which version is better, in which ways, and why, they are forced to weigh the claims of authorial intentions, editorial principles, and their own value judgments. These matters cannot be debated apart from attention to theme, structure, point of view, characterization, tone, atmosphere, versification, and language. I am always tempted to extend these freewheeling sessions by bringing in related ballads, from "Thomas Rymer" to "The Crystal Cabinet," by Blake, to "The Well-Beloved," by Hardy. As long as the focus remains on Keats's revisions, this exercise of comparison helps students develop a standard for poetic art that enhances their appreciation for other poems, especially those that depend heavily on implication rather than statement.

In even the most elementary class, the question of point of view arises— out of the air, as it were, rather than in response to the teacher's prompting: how do the poem's participants respond to the present or past situations? There are at least four points of view: that of Keats as person or as author; that of a narrator who speaks the first three stanzas, and, presumably, reports the story; that of the knight at arms, who tells his tale in the last nine stanzas (and, through him, the point of view of the pale kings and princes); and, finally, that of the lady—although that viewpoint can be inferred only from her "language strange" and ambiguous actions, as described by the knight.

Of all these, the point of view of Keats as a person is least useful pedagogically, since it depends on biographical speculations concerning his attitudes toward Fanny, his dead brother Tom, "poetry and the nature of human life . . . and a great many other things that we know nothing about"

(*Keats*, ed. Stillinger, 1982, 463–64). A teacher who chooses to pursue this question at all might wish to approach it through closely related poems such as "Ode on Melancholy," "Lamia," and especially "What can I do to drive away," that epistle composed after Keats had fallen into a distraction like that of his knight. The main reason for my own reluctance to open up this rich intertextual area of concern in Keats's work, which might also entail the slippery kisses of Endymion, is that it would take so long to study that consideration of other important poems would be precluded.

What must be established, though, is the authorial perspective on this distinctly distanced story, which took place long ago in "faery lands." Of the loss of the fairy world in modern times we need not be reminded. In view of the plight of the knight and perhaps (when we think about it) of the lady, there is no cause for nostalgia. Yet the quite vivid narrational pattern in which the uncharacterized narrator interrogates and describes the knight and his surroundings evokes the scene as clearly, as immediately, as if it were happening here and now. The effect of distance comes less from remoteness of time and place than from the author's restraint in either telling or implying what is to be made of the story, pathetic or even tragic as the situation appears. Despite the crucial element of mystery, which cannot and should not be explained away, a sense is conveyed that encounters between the sexes are all too often like that, however different this couple may have been from ordinary people in our time. The encounter between the human knight and the elfin lady seems inevitable, as does the bereavement of the knight.

The enfolding of perspectives in this narrational pattern, probably derived from Wordsworth, also resembles that of Shelley's "Ozymandias": an anonymous, featureless, almost uncharacterized narrator opens the poem and provides our only access to everything that follows. The narrator's point of view, indeed, blends with our own. We are given no information about the speaker whatsoever, not even as to gender—although the remote outdoor setting, the narrator's initiation of the conversation, and the sense of fellow feeling expressed toward the knight would suggest that the narrator is male. The questions move the ailing knight to tell his tale, and the questioner's observations of the knight and of the autumnal scene reveal the outcome before the story begins, establishing a diagrammatic contrast between the auspicious outset and the tragic conclusion. This framing task is concluded at the end of the third stanza; in the rest of the poem the initiator of the conversation disappears except as an implied audience for—and effaced transmitter of—the knight's first-person narration. The closure effected in the conclusion (46–48) is brilliantly executed in the knight's reiteration and confirmation of the narrator's observation in the opening (2–4). But the narrator does not return to offer guidance to the significance of the adventure and the resultant condition of the knight. The reader remains in a lyric relationship, overhearing the dialogue that took place centuries ago.

The knight's verbal confirmation of the opening description of his appearance and behavior does not, however, endorse the observer's pessimistic assessment of his plight. The questions about the knight's behavior are prompted by the assumption that there can be no good reason for anyone to loiter about this godforsaken place; something must be amiss. The knight's response reveals that, in his view, the memory of his extraordinary experience more than compensates for his present state of deprivation. Like an addict of the strange food and company of the fairy lady, he lingers as near as he can to where he last saw her—under the hill. That he is wasting away does not seem important; all has been worth the cost, though he now sojourns where "the sedge is wither'd from the lake, / And no birds sing" (47–48). If the knight has any regrets, they are only that his jarring dream proleptically banished him from the most satisfying relationship he could hope ever to have. He does not know the source of this exclusionary dream, nor does he care whether the warning was justified—any more than he questions whether the royal warriors had indeed been victimized by a Circe or whether they were phantasms of his own fevered imagination. He feels that he has been bereft, not that he has escaped.

The hero's state of mind would hardly be worth questioning if the 1820 *Indicator* version of the poem were adopted as the text. For there the hero is merely a "wretched wight," a poor, contemptible fellow, demeaned by the very sound of the phrase that identifies him—an epithet suited to the lips of Elmer Fudd, perhaps, but bathetic in any other context. For such a lowly person, the warning of even one king, let alone an assemblage of royal warrior-admonishers, is not only grossly disproportionate to his station in life but also a violation of the decorum established in the poem. Despite what may well be certain other structural improvements in the later version, the wretchedness of the initial designation of the hero in the revision has in itself been enough to drive generations of readers back to the 1819 text —so many, indeed, that a published exposition of the reasons for rejecting "wretched wight" has hardly been considered necessary. But should certain students—graduate students, probably, who have read François Matthey, David Simpson, or Jerome McGann—nevertheless persist in advocating the 1820 text, a remedial assignment is at hand. It would not be the standard exercise of running through the array of citations in the OED (although the passages in Scott—known to Keats—would be worth pursuing; and an interesting parallel usage that Keats would not have known, "wailing wight" in "A Dream," by Blake, not cited, is also pertinent). A more efficient pursuit would be to provide them with copies of the "wretched" and "wight" entries in Charles Grovesnor Osgood's *Spenser Concordance* and ask that these be followed up in a complete edition of Spenser. Those who do their homework will find that the dozen occurrences of "wretched wight" in Spenser usually refer either to monsters or, more often, to unfortunate women, although both the wounded Timias and Jesus during his Passion also earn the epithet. The Spenserian context will help students see that "wretched wight," even as part of the medieval idiom, is out of keeping with the characters in the dream, who were simply carried over from the first version. Keats nodded as reviser, not as creator, of this fascinating poem.

At this point the teacher may ask what kind of tale we would have if the narrator had chanced upon the lady and interviewed her (in her own strange language) instead of the knight. Most commentators write as if they already know "herstory" (although without telling what it is) or as if all we need to know of it is contained within the truncated message of the pale, victimized warriors. Others write as though the full story is unknowable and should not be probed: everything about the relationship between the knight and the lady is supposed to be mysterious. A good class can go much further: someone will begin thinking about the lady's weeping and sighing "full sore"—does this mean she also is a victim? If she spoke "in language strange," how can the knight be "sure" she really said, "I love thee true," or meant what she said? If the class is unwilling to settle for the solution imposed by commentators such as Walter Jackson Bate (*John Keats*) and Harold Bloom (*Visionary Company*)—that the secret of the poem lies in the mutual incomprehensibility of the human and fairy languages—a debate will ensue, and the poem will be scoured for evidence: how, after all, can we know that the lady really had sinister designs on the knight?

It will soon become evident that most commentators have unconsciously adopted an androcentric view of the lady—one reflecting, no doubt, elements of Keats's own well-documented inability to think of women as friends or companions, or even as people. Even those critics who have registered skepticism about the veracity of the royal characters in the dream have usually taken for granted that the lady is a mantrap, a selfish, manipulating femme fatale. Far too little attention has been paid to indications that—like Geraldine in Coleridge's "Christabel"—the lady may be as unhappy in the "elfin grot" as her lover will become outside it, perhaps from foreknowledge of the disaster to befall him or perhaps from awareness that she herself has been doomed by some powerful preternatural influence to initiate a liaison, or many liaisons, that can end only in separation and bereavement. At any rate, the knight's retrospective characterization of her, from the moment he met her, as a "faery's child" suggests that he was not deceived about her nature; apparently he was never in doubt that she belonged to another realm, another order of being. And a knight (not a "wight") should be expected to know that such companionship is perilous.

Against this line of thought, there is the title of the poem: not only is it a powerful argument against the character of the lady, but it also serves as a charm to ward off her spell over the reader. What could be said in favor of a lady "without mercy"? If she is recognized to be a beautiful lady without mercy yet (ironically) cannot be rejected as an indubitably malignant character, perhaps it would not be too farfetched to view her as a fairy champion, a defender of the old ways of her native elfin people against the invasion of an alien culture. In that context she would not be an arbitrary enchantress like Circe but would be a wily female warrior like Judith (or, from the Philistine point of view, Delilah), a person for whom feminine stratagems are the only available weapons against superior physical power. But the reader who is not an ideologue has to draw back from this potential political allegory and recognize that what has just been fabricated by critical speculation is a story that Keats might have told but didn't—though it remains, perhaps, as an overtone that can help explain why Keats's mysterious poem continues to suggest some truth about love in the world we know.

"La Belle Dame sans Merci," like *The Faerie Queene*, has the schematic characteristics of allegory; but in the assignment of values to the characters and to the deeds of the poem, it is not easy to say what stands for what. Critics with a strongly allegorical cast of mind, such as Earl R. Wasserman and especially Mario L. D'Avanzo, have argued, against a near consensus of other readers, that the encounter with the lady is supposed to be a good thing and that it is the expulsion from her company that is unfortunate. D'Avanzo even maintains that the lady is the muse and the hero is a poet who cannot sustain an imaginative experience. If a student, prompted or unprompted by D'Avanzo, should propose this view of the relationship, it would be the concern of the rest of the class to test the theory rather than to refute it. Such an allegorical impulse at least grows out of the premise that the poem as a whole was designed to mean something. To this extent it is preferable to symbolist or poststructural exegeses that deliberate inconclusively about several symbols or words and then declare that the poem is "about uncertainty."

In courses in allegory or semiotics it would be profitable to study "La Belle Dame sans Merci" in connection with the 1953 film *Ugetsu*, directed by Kenji Mizoguchi, which was based on eighteenth-century stories by Ueda; the scene of the encounter between a "wretched wight" of a hero and the charming femme fatale could hardly be better imagined. Or, Keats's poem can be studied with allegorical pictures of the Renaissance: Dürer's related pair of engravings known as *Young Lady on Horseback and Lansquenet* (1497) and *Young Couple Threatened by Death* (1498) and Raphael's *Dream of a Knight* (1504). The Raphael painting (now in the National Gallery, London) is particularly apt, since it came to London in 1801 and might well

have been seen by Keats, a self-professed Raphael enthusiast, in company
with his friend B. R. Haydon, who had a reputation as the modern Raphael.
One of the two ladies dreamed of by Raphael's knight is La Belle Dame,
and in the background is the "elfin grot."[1] In any case, the centrality of "La
Belle Dame sans Merci" is such that almost any classroom comment or
published commentary can be directed toward some major aspect of the
work and toward a major issue in the interpretation of poetry. That is why,
if the teacher can avoid instruction, the poem lends itself so well to education.[2]

NOTES

[1]The Dürer engravings, *Young Lady* and *Young Couple*, are reproduced in Strauss,
plates 18 and 20. Raphael's still more suggestive *Dream of the Knight*—it has been
given several other titles—was owned by W. Y. Ottley; if Keats saw this wonderful
little picture, a recollection of it could have prompted "La Belle Dame sans Merci."
The lady who tempts the sleeping knight with a posy and pearls is balanced by
another lady who tempts with a sword (as well as a book), the implement of the pale
regal warriors who disrupt the complacency of Keats's knight. Keats could not have
seen an engraving of this picture, since apparently none was made before the 1830s;
Pezzini et al. provides an exceptionally clear reproduction that is actually larger than
the picture itself (entry 262, pl. 834). A good color reproduction, slightly reduced,
appears in Jones and Penny 6. The standard catalog in English is Dussler.

[2]After I wrote the foregoing essay, I read Karen Swann's chapter in Anne K.
Mellor's *Romanticism and Feminism* and the second chapter in Majorie Levinson's
1988 book. I found myself wondering whether either would find anything significantly
different to say about John Suckling's "Why So Pale and Wan, Fond Lover?" Students
who read either of these accounts might be interested to speculate about this question.

Student "Experts" Teaching Keats's Odes

Frank Jordan

One of the most appealing features of Romantic poetry to undergraduates, even to freshmen and sophomores in introductory surveys of British literature, is the call for creative response or imaginative participation by the reader. Wordsworth invokes it explicitly in poems like "Lines Left upon a Seat in a Yew-Tree," "Simon Lee," "The Ruined Cottage," and "Hart-Leap Well" and in the 1800 Preface to *Lyrical Ballads*; Coleridge summons the active reader throughout his poetry and prose but most especially in *The Friend*. Karl Kroeber, in *British Romantic Art*, is at pains to make the Romantic artist's concern for the audience's "participative re-creativeness" (1) the distinctive feature of Romanticism:

> Romanticism's most fundamental commitments . . . assure that it cannot be an isolated aesthetic movement, nor can it define itself adequately through *simple* antagonism to prevailing social mores. At its most intensely personal moments of exploration and expression Romantic art engages itself with the problematics of its potential audience's response.
>
> (29)

In a recent survey course, given a choice of nine topics for an hour exam on Romanticism, most students selected the one about the reader's role in Romantic poetry. It is not surprising perhaps that, in this instance, quantity and quality went hand in hand: those same students also wrote the best exams.

The suggestion I put forward here for teaching Keats's odes is intended not for a survey course, however, but for an advanced undergraduate course in the second-generation Romantics. The approach need not, though, be limited to that course. Indeed, I also recommend it for a course devoted to the first-generation Romantic poets, where one might reserve for papers a poem each by Blake, Wordsworth, and Coleridge—say, "The Book of Thel," the "Intimations" ode, and "Christabel." In the sequel course, however, typically populated at my university by juniors, seniors, and a few belated graduate students making up deficiencies, I usually ask students to write on one of Keats's odes. How many of the poems I reserve for these papers depends on the size of the class, but I always use at least three—"Ode to a Nightingale," "Ode on a Grecian Urn," and "To Autumn." Since Keats is the last writer we take up, devoting the final meetings to the odes satisfies the claims of both chronology and aesthetics.

Long before the papers are due, I divide the class up more or less evenly on the odes, working from ranked lists of students' preferences solicited several days in advance. The requirement is that each student write a ten-to-twelve-page interpretation of an ode, bringing as much creativity and imagination to bear as possible. The expectation is not that they will do exhaustive research but that they will have read widely enough in the criticism to have perspective on their interpretations—to have a context for estimating their own originality as well as Keats's. In large part the purpose is to prepare them to defend their interpretations against challenges from classmates on the day given over to discussing their ode. In addition, they become aware of the principal issues and critical cruxes that have attracted the attention of professional scholars. Thus the students write as Keats claimed, after completing *Endymion*, that he would write henceforth—"independently & *with* judgment" (*Letters* 1: 374). Their creative response to the poem is, in other words, an informed one. On the day their papers are due, all the students who have written on the same ode form a panel of "experts" whose responsibility is to field questions from the other members of the class, who have read the ode of the day but not read about or written about it. On subsequent days, when other odes are featured, the panelists become the audience and vice versa. Students could, of course, collaborate on a paper, but in my experience they resist that idea. Though they are not averse to sharing information and seem to relish talking about their poem with others, they prefer to write their own papers. The advantage of individual papers is the likelihood of highly divergent interpretations, not to mention multiform approaches and eccentric emphases. Even a small group of students who have concentrated on a single lyric can generate a wealth of information and variety of viewpoint. To be sure, they will use ideas from earlier discussions, but their preparation for these panels makes them confident enough to offer independent views and even to be dogged in defending them. Sometimes the panelists argue so intently among themselves that members of the audience have to compete for their attention.

It is important, I think, not to let the experts begin by reading or even summarizing their papers. Rather, I indicate in advance that I will choose a member of the audience to start the meeting by asking a question—the more specific the better—about the ode under discussion and that I will urge that individual not to let go of the question until satisfied with the answer. (I also stress that I will not again open my mouth unless there is a lull in the discussion, whereupon I will call on a member of the audience to pose another question.) Lest the students not on the panel think their role in these meetings is secondary, I instruct them to read the poems carefully (panelists may, after all, turn a question back on the questioner) and come prepared with written questions—lots of them in case someone else asks the same questions. I recommend, too, that students be prepared to elaborate on their questions—to phrase them in different ways—in order to improve their chances for good answers. "Be prepared and be persistent" best sums up the protocol of the meetings for the audience.

My advice to the panelists is twofold: first, take the initiative in answering a question, particularly if it is not addressed to someone else—or, if it is, supplement the answer or, if possible, quarrel with it; second, be generous in sharing your knowledge (from your research) and your understanding (from your thinking). Undergraduates seem fascinated by disagreement among professional interpreters, and they are not loath, if encouraged, to air their opinions and to take sides.

Finally, I emphasize that the grade for the assignment is based on the paper, participation as panelist, and participation as member of the audience. And I tell a few cautionary tales from previous years about people who, as panelists or audience members, held back only to discover that the hour was over and the opportunity to take part lost.

More often than not these classes prove too short, especially from the vantage point of the students, who leave the room drained but exhilarated, wishing "every class could be like this." (I smile and refrain from saying the obvious, namely, that if they invested as much of themselves in every class as they had in this one, then it would be.)

These class meetings can be used to generate examination questions not only on Keats but on Romantic literature in general. Some of the speculations and queries about Romanticism that inevitably arise in the panel sessions can be turned to good effect, especially if in the exam students are permitted to assume that Keats is representative and to draw heavily on him for illustrative material. A recent series of meetings on the odes, for example, revealed that students, both in their papers and in their discussion, were preoccupied with the problem of endings for writers and readers of Romantic poetry—and keen on the notion of sharing with the poet the responsibility for completing the poem. For the final exam, therefore, I quoted lines 65–68 of Wordsworth's "Simon Lee":

> O Reader! had you in your mind
> Such stores as silent thought can bring,
> O gentle Reader! you would find
> A tale in every thing.

I then wrote: "One message to emerge from our last three meetings is that endings are problematic for Romantic poets or their readers or both. Why should this be so? What is the tale of Romanticism to be found by the thoughtful in Romantic endings? Make a tale of it." Alternatively, one might from the beginning reserve a poem or two of Byron's and of Shelley's (particularly "Ode to the West Wind") along with some odes of Keats's and use the special meetings as a review of the entire course, which is then completed by a comprehensive exam. Whatever the plan, the paper-cum-panel exercise is in my experience the best way to end the term with a bang and to show students, especially those nearing graduation, that they have learned the secret of education—namely, to be their own teachers. The exercise is also healthy for the teacher, who does well to cultivate something of the Grecian urn's unrivaled capacity for the response of silence. Like Keats in that poem, the students in this exercise are thrown back on themselves; they must ultimately answer their own questions. Romantic poetry is an exceptionally felicitous means to that end.

Keats with a Lifetime Warranty

Brian Wilkie

My teaching of Keats—about a quarter century of it—indicates that he is, by a wide margin, the most popular with students of the English Romantic poets. Wordsworth and Coleridge are blue-chip authors with stable, perennial appeal. Byron, at the other extreme, remains a special taste, even in classes fortunate enough not to have an instructor who disdains him. The stock of Blake and Shelley fluctuates considerably in tandem with such things as mind expansion and purportedly revolutionary consciousness. Even in the most favorable circumstances, however, all five of these other poets need to be sold, pushed, preached. Keats alone seems to teach himself, to capture students' imaginations strongly and immediately. Group explication of his work is a pleasure; for all his richness and the elusiveness of his symbolic imagery, students sense from the outset the larger patterns of his thought, and even those students most resistant to subtlety of interpretation seem disarmed of their suspiciousness and ready to "read things in" with the rest of us. On papers and examinations, Keats tends not infrequently to turn good students into especially articulate ones and to activate a vein of imagination even in stolid minds.

If all this is even roughly true, it will doubtless seem perverse to find anything disturbing in the situation. Nevertheless, I for one am a little—or more than a little—disturbed. A Carolinian of my acquaintance once defined southern cuisine with the succinct formula "It slides down." The same can often be said of Keats's poetry. And that, I submit, is not a very good thing.

Seen close up, the problem is that students' responses seem to slip effortlessly into certain predictable grooves; given freedom to choose their topics on papers or examinations, almost all of them gravitate toward one of two matters: life versus art, and idealist escapism versus realist confrontation of pain. So far so good, perhaps, since these are the central issues in Keats; still, one would expect a poet with such a fine and comprehensive intellect to enter students' minds by channels more various. More important, however, is that students find easy ways out: the art-life conflict is judged a draw, each alternative having its advantages (as if human beings could choose whether to live in the flesh or as painted figures on an urn!). The hedonism-pain conflict is resolved by a kind of Panglossian formula: pain is an inevitable and even healthy element in life without which we could not appreciate pleasure or beauty. (Incidentally, it is difficult, in our age of ecological models of nature, for students to get worked up about the "eternal fierce destruction" in which fish and robins are engaged in Keats's verse epistle to Reynolds. But that is a special case.)

A more serious problem is that students, despite their initial enthusiasm, appear not to retain Keats as a touchstone of later growth. A Romanticist friend recently mentioned to me that, while former students occasionally tell him how Blake, for example, has been enriched by their experience or has enriched it, he never gets analogous reports about Keats. This has been my experience too. It isn't that students later dislike Keats; rather, as a spiritual resource he wears only indifferently well, as though he had come with only a one- or two-year warranty. Unlike Blake or Wordsworth or Coleridge or even Shelley, he does not become a permanent element in the chemistry of students' consciousness and values.

It may seem that I am resuscitating the old argument about whether Keats's poetry conveys ideas. And perhaps that issue is pertinent here. Romanticists, particularly Keatsians, like to point out that, even in the hostile anti-Romantic atmosphere of the New Criticism, Keats retained an honored place among poets. When we consider, however, that Shakespeare and Milton also took some beatings during the New Critics' ascendancy, we may wonder whether Keats's untouchableness was not attributable less to his excellence than to his harmlessness. But this question is not the most crucial one in my context. Even if Keats is not a poet of ideas, that fact does not explain his failure to play a lasting part in the spiritual development of students, for surely it is a writer's stance toward life, the mythic dimension of his or her work, that counts in this respect, not the inherent philosophical content of the ideas expressed. Moreover, for some important writers, including Yeats, Stevens, and Scott Fitzgerald, Keats did remain a permanent force and benchmark. That, mutatis mutandis, this tends not to be true for our students, even those for whom literature remains a vital focus of their values, is not Keats's fault but ours as teachers. Keats's work is inherently a poetry of sharp challenge, and there is no reason why it must become less challenging as years elapse. Our failing is that we allow Keats's poetry to "slide down." Rather, we should be forcing our students to half-choke on it, dramatizing in our classrooms the existentially disturbing matters that Keats faced up to but that our students evade and defuse.

The "Ode on Melancholy" provides one of the clearest examples of what can go wrong in the teaching and learning of Keats. This poem is an agonized cri de coeur, and yet students commonly shy away from the implications of that cry. Instead of sharing Keats's bitterness over the obscene fact that what is beautiful must die, students are prone to devise a silver-lining solution: if the death of beauty is the surest occasion for melancholy, then, on the same evidence, a dash of melancholy is a healthy part of experience—indeed, a gourmet seasoning for our encounters with what is beautiful in life. That may be true (Keats himself wobbled on the question whether it was the sign of a healthy mind to mingle sadness with joy), but so invertebrate a conclusion surely deprives the "Melancholy" ode of its shattering power, the kind of power that should make the poem sink into students' souls to be tested in their present and future lives.

The same kind of complacency can lull readers of other poems by Keats, so that his paradoxes, which ought to threaten to tear us apart, become instead an invitation to establish a merely well-adjusted personality—like that of Keats, students may feel, who was so admirably capable of seeing both sides of things. Enduring forever on an urn, joining a nightingale in a never-never land, living with one's lover in a palace of sweet sin—all these have their appeal, but "real life" (a phrase students tend maddeningly to use as if it clearly meant anything) has its pleasures too. I am reminded of what Lionel Trilling said of his students in modern-literature courses: "I asked them to look into the Abyss, and, both dutifully and gladly, they have looked into the Abyss, and the Abyss has greeted them with . . . grave courtesy . . ." (*Beyond Culture* 27).

How, in practical terms of classroom teaching, do we encourage students to take Keats's issues with the sense of urgency they deserve? Two decades ago, in the heyday of audience-involvement theater, I saw a cartoon: two spear-carrying ancient Egyptians prowl the aisles of an opera house, fixing the bland audience with scowls and withering scorn: "You don't even care, do you, that Radames and Aida are dying by suffocation." Applied to teaching Keats, that method—of frenzied exhortation—would be lame. A more effective method is to get students to argue with one another. It is a procedure I have applied to the teaching of many authors and works, but it seems especially useful for Keats.

A week or so before teaching a particular work—the "Melancholy" ode, perhaps, or "The Eve of St. Agnes"—I select four students to lead a panel discussion on a pertinent question. This question must be answered yes or no. I deliberately frame questions that are blunt to the point sometimes of simplemindedness: "Is melancholy, as Keats describes it, a good thing?" "Is the love scene in 'The Eve of St. Agnes' selfish escapism?" (One could, alternatively, frame more concrete questions, such as "Are the words 'No, no' at the beginning of the 'Melancholy' ode sarcastic?") As with debate teams, students are assigned a position, affirmative or negative, that they must argue regardless of their personal views. They are not permitted to take "maybe" or "in some ways" positions. They must make an opening statement, *in no more than one minute*, after which they must engage the other panel members in debate. After ten minutes or so of such debate, the question is thrown open to general discussion by the entire class. Unlike the panelists, the class at large has the option of fence-straddling yes-and-no answers. These debates are more likely to become fervent if the panelists do not meet in advance to plan or rehearse; preparation would blunt the keen edge of encounter and tone down extreme positions.

Despite the fussiness of the format, these sessions often produce heated discussion. Equally important, when poems by Keats are the subject, the debates are likely to turn on questions of poetic tone and the strategies by which that tone is conveyed. (For example, the words "No, no" can be understood in any of eight or so different tones.) And surely it is through the awareness of tone that the real power and emotional thrust of Keats's poems are most deeply felt. To the extent that the line "Then glut thy sorrow on a morning rose" is taken as more or less straight-faced, the "Melancholy" ode is a Panglossian poem. If the line conveys, instead, desperation or a panicky disgust at the need to snatch pleasure from the jaws of death and dissolution, the poem becomes one of the most memorable of tragic statements.

This method can be used with almost all Keats's important short poems and some medium-length ones, such as "The Eve of St. Agnes." It is also suitable for the other poems, if one is willing to forgo the close examination of tone that I have been emphasizing. I am not sure it would work with "Lamia," since that poem contains its own discursive arguments for and against the love affair and thus calls less for discussion than for a vote on evidence already, in substance, presented. But perhaps this is just an admission of my own limitation; I must confess to finding "Lamia" the most intractable of Keats's poems, to teach or to understand at all.

Earlier in this essay I made a broader confession: that I am among those teachers who have been less than successful in instilling even in good students a lasting sense of Keats's profound value as a touchstone for experience. To those teachers who may have been more successful, I apologize for visiting on them the sins of which only some of us are guilty.

Keatsian Turns:
Diagraming Metaphor and Empathy

Bruce Clarke

A Poet . . . has no Identity—he is continually in for—
and filling some other Body. . . . But even now I am
perhaps not speaking from myself; but from some
character in whose soul I now live.

Keats, *Letters*

The premise of my remarks is that by approaching the teaching of Keats's poetry through some of the basic structures of language and metaphor, you can use Keats's poems to advantage as an introduction to poetic language in general.

First of all, you might remind the class that words are both denotative and connotative (see fig. 1). They both denote specific meanings, ideas, and images and evoke other meanings, ideas, and images, along with the feelings a reader attaches to them. (I offer throughout the essay diagrams that I share with students to clarify this approach.)

From their composition courses, your students may be familiar with another distinction—that between exposition and persuasion. Whereas expository writing demands precise denotations, persuasive writing exploits connotative values, mixing expository and exhortatory language in order to press particular concrete appeals. Since the aim of persuasive rhetoric is not only to inform but to evoke feeling-toned attitudes, it is already halfway to poetic writing. In poetry, however, the immediate practical ends of both exposition and persuasion are put aside, while the evocation and movement of connotative meaning become primary. The immediate point is that the meanings of poetic language are found mostly beneath the line of definition and denotation. So poetry must be read between the lines, where connotative values become metaphorical movements of meaning among words. For a diagram of metaphor, I adapt I. A. Richards's famous distinction between "tenor" and "vehicle," that is, between the general complex of value and feeling associated with a verbal trope and the concrete term that embodies or evokes that complex (see fig. 2).

Words are complex. The poet sets their complexities into action by making metaphors, or turns of phrase. In figure 2, one word is explicitly or implicitly linked to another in a figurative relation, a reciprocal turn, so that the dominant quality of one term is carried over to the other. You might say that a metaphor is a bargain the poet has two words strike, a swap or seizure of semantic possessions. The arrows indicate the movements of significance in a typical metaphor: the feeling of the tenor imbues the idea of the vehicle; and the vehicle is chosen because its idea evokes the feeling of the tenor.

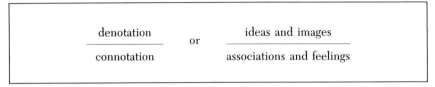

Figure 1. Word

For instance, in the first line of "Ode on a Grecian Urn," "Thou" is the tenor of a complex figure and at the same time the vehicle of a previous metaphor, motivated by the poet's primal turn, the personification of the urn (see fig. 3). The poet sets us forth on the path of his personification, not by denoting any literal details of the urn but by using a series of vehicles that associate it with a particular set of human attributes. The urn is a "bride," an image combining ideas of vulnerability, modesty, and anticipation, which are then transferred back to the urn. Implicitly, we are asked to show the urn the courtesy and solicitude we would show a young bride. We are invited to imagine a figurative maidenhood almost but never quite forgone. When the "leaf-fringed legend" painted on the urn comes into focus in stanza 2, another beloved figure appears, eternally suspended just beyond her "Bold lover."

What makes Keats especially rewarding for the study of personification is that his poetic personae enter fully into the projective and receptive devices of metaphor, what Paul de Man has described as "the representation, the dramatization, in terms of the experience of a subject, of a rhetorical structure" (*Allegories* 13). In other words, the play of poetic language underwrites the play of the imagination: Keats shows clearly how the empathetic imagination is structured like the turnings of metaphor, how the forms of romantic consciousness conform to the writing and reading of poetic figures.

Lyrics like the "Urn" and "Ode to a Nightingale" are metaphorical, not only from line to line but also in the whole of their larger movements. As set forth in my diagrams, Keatsian "empathy" is also a kind of turn, but this existential turn is the reciprocal of the motions described in "metaphor." In both poems the poet's persona is positioned as a poetic tenor to which the "object" (poem) is predicated as poetic vehicle (see fig. 4).

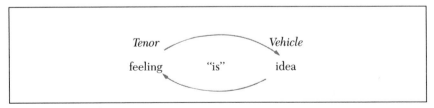

Figure 2. Metaphor

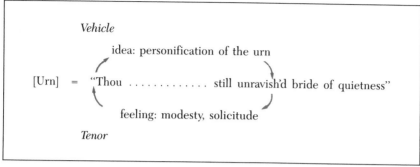

Figure 3. Personification

In this schema, the poem as a whole performs an empathetic turn. The poet prefigures all the particular figures of the poem by investing his subjective position in the inanimate object. Thus, at the end of stanza 1, the "wild ecstasy" that the poet depicts on the side of the urn also describes the mode of the persona: the poet has become ecstatic, has gone out of his own place to assume the urn's position. In stanzas 2–4, the poet measures the effects of that self-projection, that "sacrifice" of self on the altar of poetic compassion. Our sketch helps us see that the notes of emptiness and desolation in stanza 4 refer fundamentally to the poet himself, whose ecstasy purchases a participation with another's essence at the price of an extreme vulnerability and self-forgetting. Stanza 5 re-turns the poet from his perilous journey into the vehicle back to the position of the tenor, reestablishes differences, and redefines the proprieties of this relation: "Thou, silent form, dost tease us out of thought." Keats's interaction with the urn is like a dance, composed of movements of approach and departure, and like an echo of the romance depicted on the urn: "She cannot fade, though thou hast not thy bliss." In its whole movement, the "Urn" traces a dialectical spiral (see fig. 5).

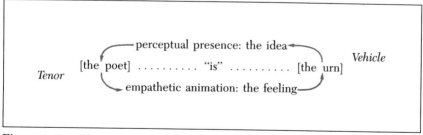

Figure 4. Empathy

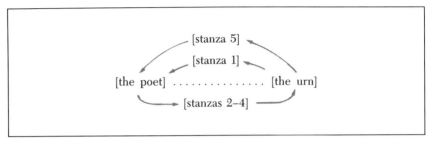

Figure 5. The empathetic career in the "Urn"

If we place the "Nightingale" alongside the "Urn," we can see that both poems are concerned with the courtesies and the faux pas of empathetic circulation. With the urn, the poet confronts an inanimate vehicle, a cultural artifact. But with the nightingale the poet encounters a natural being, a living thing. Whereas the immobile urn presents itself visually, the winged nightingale is invisible and pours out its "full-throated" presence in birdsong. Stanzas 1 and 2 revolve around images of containers that tend to equate the poet's persona with his own vehicles. The body of the persona and the beaker are both vessels of spirits: in stanza 1 the poet absorbs and succumbs to the bird's song, and in stanza 2 the "beaker full of the warm South" holds a vintage that induces a pleasant yet morbid intoxication. The listening self, the receptacle of the nightingale's intoxicating song, is also a violated orifice, a "purple-stained mouth."

The format of the "Nightingale"—the aural voluptuousness, the backyard garden instead of the dim museum—lets Keats dwell in a more leisurely way on the minutiae of the particular empathetic career being enacted (see fig. 6). This transport is carried on "viewless wings," not just by the invisible wings of metaphor but also by an imagination that discovers itself in its trance nearly sightless: "no light . . . I cannot see . . . embalmed darkness." The ecstatic consciousness, nearly dissolved in sounds, smells, and sensuous guesses (st. 5), is immersed in the medium of connotation and unable to denote. It must pull its identity together through thoughts of "easeful Death" (st. 6) and in doing so is reminded of the mortality of its "sole self" even before the word "Forlorn!" tolls at the beginning of stanza 8. Here again, the wandering imagination remembers itself by way of images of desolation and displacement.

Stanza 7 beautifully evokes the sense of alienation through the figure of Ruth. Like the Grecian urn, Ruth is also a vulnerable exile, a homesick bride. With Ruth, moreover, the poet has finally gathered the projective energies of the poem toward a specific human figure. The nightingale may then be said to develop into a series of opposed personifications, first the masculine duo of "emperor and clown," then the feminine pair of Ruth and

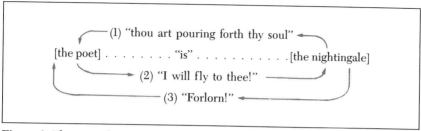

Figure 6. The empathetic career in the "Nightingale"

the "deceiving elf," the "fancy." In Keats's poetry as a whole, similar inter-
plays between sympathetic and demonic personae recur both within poems,
as here in the "Nightingale" between Ruth and the "fancy," and from one
poem to another: for instance, the alternations among sympathetic figures
like Madeline and Psyche and demonic figures such as La Belle Dame sans
Merci. It is in fact the unresolved but productive presence of both the
sympathetic and the demonic projections of this poetic self that accounts for
the power of Keats's Lamia, a character who is at once lost soul and deceptive
temptress.

I have tried to suggest some discussions one could generate from these
diagrams of metaphor and empathy and to indicate how one might move
from the "Urn" and the "Nightingale" to other poems by Keats. In addition,
one might then study "The Rime of the Ancient Mariner" or *A Midsummer
Night's Dream* and examine the structural parallels between Keats's mi-
crodramas of figurative participation and the circular plots of Coleridge's
poem and Shakespeare's drama. Like those works, both the "Urn" and the
"Nightingale" are based on excursion-and-return models that play lyrically
and ironically on comic and romantic expectations: departure, trial, and
reunion; spiritual quest; epiphanic experience. In sum, the dynamics of
metaphor, so vivid in Keats's particular practice, can provide students with
contexts for comprehending the larger formal energies and conventional
patterns of poetic texts.

Keats's Politics of Truth

Lore Metzger

Students of Keats, whether stressing his idealism or realism, frequently speak the same critical language and operate with the same critical norms. That good poems are self-contained, organically coherent, complexly articulated structures is a New Critical version of Romantic poetics that, despite serious challenges from deconstructionists and others, has remained entrenched among leading Romanticists. From M. H. Abrams and Walter Jackson Bate to Jack Stillinger and Helen Vendler, the normative assumption has been perpetuated that Murray Krieger, a sympathetic opponent of New Criticism, formulated in 1965: "Central to a poem's becoming successfully poetic . . . is the poem's achieving a formal and linguistic self-sufficiency . . . [that] involves the poem's coming to terms with itself, its creating the sense of roundedness" (105). Not without cause did Jerome McGann in 1983 charge, "Today the scholarship and interpretation of Romantic works is dominated by an uncritical absorption in Romanticism's own self-representations." Especially prominent is an uncritical absorption in the Romantic view that the divisions, conflicts, and dislocations of English society in that period "can only be resolved beyond the realm of immediate experience, at the level of the mind's idea or the heart's desire . . . and hence that poetry by its nature can transcend the conflicts and transiences of this time and that place" (McGann, *Romantic Ideology* 137, 69).

As teachers we tend to proselytize and to privilege as a humanistic heritage the special insights we gain from Romantic poetry. As for Keats, the letters included in the most widely used paperback texts clearly invite us to teach his poetry in the context of his aesthetic or psychological concerns and to apply to his poetry his belief in the authenticity of the imagination or in the efficacy of negative capability. But shouldn't we also show our students how to read his poems not only sympathetically and respectfully but also skeptically and irreverently? Shouldn't we move beyond aestheticizing Keats and break down the barriers separating poetry (and all purely literary studies) from the other texts (social, economic, or political) that inform our world as they informed Keats's?

In recent years I have experimented with teaching Keats and the other Romantic poets first from a formalistic and empathic perspective, modeled on Cleanth Brooks's reading of the "Ode on a Grecian Urn"; I have then challenged my students to produce a more distanced, critical review and revaluation and to supplement (without supplanting) traditional thematic and formalistic concerns with questions about the ideological implications of Romantic norms. I offer here a discussion of the "Ode to a Nightingale" to demonstrate the kind of critical analysis in which my current teaching is grounded.

Critics traditionally question the paradoxical implications of the poet's flight "on the viewless wings of Poesy" to leave the painful world of heartache and death and to achieve imaginative identification with the timeless aesthetic realm of the nightingale. The most influential framework for discussion, Abrams's paradigm of the greater Romantic lyric, emphasizes a colloquy between subject and object, in which the speaker is led to a deepened understanding or a resolution of a moral or psychological problem ("Structure" 527–28). In discussing the "Ode to a Nightingale," which, according to Abrams, approximates the paradigm more closely than any of Keats's other odes, the critic-teacher raises questions about the status of the object (the nightingale) that evokes the speaker's self-probing, longing for oblivion, and, finally, doubts about the entire dramatized experience. How should we interpret the retrospective reflection: "Was it a vision, or a waking dream? / Fled is that music:—Do I wake or sleep?"

Discussion of the ode within such a thematic framework leads to close reading of the text and a comparison with the other odes of 1819, laying the necessary groundwork for any further critical analysis. But reading Keats's ode as a paradigmatic greater Romantic lyric needs to be supplemented by reading it as a lyric written in 1819 rather than in 1798. A latecomer to the Romantic pantheon, Keats engages dialogically the norms and forms received from the paradigmatic lyrics of Coleridge and Wordsworth. To foreground Keats's critical experimentation with the Wordsworthian poetry of the "human heart, the main region of his song" (*Letters* 1: 279) can be the critic's first step in practicing critical distance from Romantic norms and attending to Keats's search for a Wordsworthian mode that does not have a palpable design on the reader. Keats evolves a Romantic empathy combined with irony in his greater lyrics as in his narratives. As he said of his (in his view flawed) practice in "Isabella": "in my dramatic capacity I enter fully into the feeling: but in Propria Persona I should be apt to quiz it myself" (*Letters* 2: 174).

Keats's self-criticism can alert us to the complex role his "I" plays in the "Ode to a Nightingale," incorporating both the dramatic and the "proper" personae. Precisely the ambiguity of the "I" signals Keats's radical complication of the Wordsworthian moment of doubt, which for Wordsworth intensifies affirmation, not negation. In "Tintern Abbey," for example, the moment of doubt—"If this / Be but a vain belief" (49–50)—instantly generates positive contradiction: "yet, oh! how oft . . . / O sylvan Wye! thou wanderer thro' the woods, / How often has my spirit turned to thee!" (50, 56–57). The unambiguous, authoritative voice of Wordsworth's autobiographical persona is unmistakable. But in Keats's ode the intermingling of dramatic and autobiographical voices undercuts any such authoritative gesture.

"Darkling" the speaker listens to the nightingale's ecstatic song, this spontaneous art produced with "full-throated ease." But even in the first dramatic evocation of the bird as denatured and mythicized "light-winged Dryad of the trees," the speaker is doubtful about the boundary that separates the nightingale's transcendent realm from the speaker's real spot of time. The nightingale usurps the speaker's poetic power by an aesthetic perfection defined by what it excludes: laborious artistry as well as the Philomela impulse of giving utterance to personal suffering.

As the speaker is constantly tolled back to his autobiographical self, the text is less a tribute to the nightingale, pure art unburdened by human misery, than a presentation of what the apostrophized ideal art excludes. The speaker's longing to "fade away" into the wordless realm of the nightingale ironically generates a narrative triggered by the word *fade*, a narrative that makes present precisely what the speaker wishes to dissolve into absence:

> Fade far away, dissolve, and quite forget
>   What thou among the leaves hast never known,
> The weariness, the fever, and the fret
>   Here, where men sit and hear each other groan;
> Where palsy shakes a few, sad, last gray hairs,
>   Where youth grows pale, and spectre-thin, and dies;
> Where but to think is to be full of sorrow. . . .

This catalog thus produces a highly ambiguous account of experiences unknowable to the nightingale, which is distinguished by its wordless negation of what fills the speaker's sole self with sorrow.

We might ask whether Keats's strategy of negation itself undermines the structure of the greater Romantic lyric. His strategy exposes the lyric's paradigmatic circularity as a formal accomplishment that circumscribes what is sayable and contains the problem to be resolved. Consider, for example, Wordsworth's handling of the date in the subtitle of "Tintern Abbey," 13 July 1798, which recalls a historic moment of public and personal import, the anniversary eve of Bastille Day. Relegating the date to the subtitle makes it exorbitant (in Derrida's sense) and displaces its associations from the beautifully contoured lyric text. In contrast, Keats, while continuing the Wordsworthian tradition of autobiographical dramatic self-exploration, distances himself from its palpable rhetorical design. His borders are less heavily fortified against intruding personal and social distresses. When Keats's "Nightingale" catalog of the miseries entailed in the act of thinking is compared with Wordsworth's

> In darkness and amid the many shapes
> Of joyless daylight; when the fretful stir
> Unprofitable, and the fever of the world
> Have hung upon the beatings of my heart. . . .
>   (51–54)

—a fretful stir readily calmed by the re-creative scenic memory—the younger poet's undercutting of the Wordsworthian rhetoric of containment becomes notable.

What is true about Keats's erecting ineffective barriers against personal distress is also true of his speaker's not vigilantly guarding against the invasion of unsettling social events. Once more making a dramatic move to envision the nightingale's immortal song, the speaker briefly returns to its fortunate innocence of human events: "No hungry generations tread thee down"—a statement paratactically linked to instances from the remote past that evince the presence of the immortal song. Unlike Wordsworth, who transports distressing social echoes across the lyric's borders, Keats permits their uneasy presence within the confines of his lyric. This inclusion measures his distance from the Wordsworthian lyric design, showing its limits without deconstructing them. Keats furthermore suppresses the Wordsworthian balancing of wise insights against emotional losses; he suggests no antidotes for either unpreventable suffering (the wasting away of youth) or preventable disaster (mass hunger). Keats does not deconstruct the containing boundaries of the greater Romantic lyric, since he touches on the fact of "hungry generations" only marginally, without pressing its political implications in the manner of his denunciation of "money bags" and "ledger men" in "Isabella." He subsumes the theme of hunger under the more prominently emerging themes of exile and alienation that link the autobiographical persona with Ruth. Stationing Ruth "amid the alien corn," Keats subtly alludes to her marginality as a despised foreigner who shares in the harvest's abundance only by gleaning the leavings. At the same time he incorporates her into his romantic narrative of art's ability to produce communion and community, no matter how tenuously they may function for isolated, "forlorn" individuals across the ages.

In the end the poet unmakes even this marginal community. Reading the ode's concluding stanza in the light of the Romantic lyric's much praised formal device of the return upon itself, we should take our clue from Keats's questioning of inherited norms and valorized forms: "A Question is the best beacon towards a little Speculation" (*Letters* 1: 175). And on such a beacon toward speculation he ends the "Ode to a Nightingale."

The poet who has tracked the "plaintive anthem" fading past nearby meadows and hills announces that "now 'tis buried deep / In the next valley-glades." The word *fades* ironically makes the idealized song perform the act the depressed poet had desired through the nightingale's agency—to "leave the world unseen, / And with thee fade away into the forest dim: / Fade far away. . . ." Now the nightingale's song itself dissolves and leaves the poet in an empty space that he can no longer fill with compensatory words as he had earlier filled the darkness by naming invisible flowers. The final line paratactically joins a statement and a question: "Fled is that music:—Do I wake or sleep?" If the question obliquely recalls the speaker's "drowsy numbness" of the opening stanza, it does so without resolving any problems or yielding any powerful insights. It is in fact a gesture of what Tilottama Rajan (in another context) calls "authorial abdication" (*Dark Interpreter* 101). And it may be seen as a questioning of the Romantic lyric's return upon itself, which, according to Abrams, is a "deliberate endeavor to transform a segment of experience broken out of time into a sufficient aesthetic whole" ("Structure" 532). For if art born of immortal ecstasy, of aesthetic autonomy, can fade into nonexistence when it is most needed by the mortal listener, what powerful truth can be imputed to it? Keats has tested the limits of the greater Romantic lyric and made visible its artifice of containment.

If Keats does not deconstruct the Romantic lyric's preoccupation with self-exploration, which pushes social issues to the margins of its discourse, whose interests are served by this poetic strategy? To answer this question, we might look at the most influential periodical of the time, *Blackwood's Edinburgh Magazine*, which similarly emphasized self-reflexive mental processes. In an important series of articles between 1817 and 1820, *Blackwood's* elaborated an ideology of the power of the mind as part of its campaign to legitimate the ideals of the mercantile class, its targeted audience. *Blackwood's* propagated a cultural politics that in its validation of productive genius advanced the ideal of the entrepreneur as the creator of economic progress, while at the same time assuring its middle-class readers that their ideals, their interests were also those of "common men." It cultivated the illusion of stability and universality precisely at a time when the rift between classes was becoming apparent everywhere, when observers like Wordsworth lamented the erasure of the old interdependence of classes bound together by "moral cement." In 1817 Wordsworth recognized that "the principal ties which kept the different classes of society in a vital and harmonious dependence upon each other have, within these 30 years either been greatly impaired or wholly dissolved" (*Letters* 375). *Blackwood's* offered a similar diagnosis in 1820:

> Never in any age or country was there so firm an alliance betwixt the higher and lower orders as there existed in Great Britain, until it was fatally disturbed of late years by . . . the spirit of turbulence and

faction; . . . the cord has been snapped by the revolt of the labouring classes from their natural protectors and best friends. . . .

(Qtd. in Perkin 213)

Another example of *Blackwood's* "project of imperializing mental energy" (Klancher 188) is an article in 1820, "On the Analogy between the Growth of Individual and National Genius." The author insists that there is "a just and true sympathy in common men, with that condition of the mind in which its highest faculties are best exerted—a sympathy of no ordinary moment" because it constitutes the freedom of the power of the mind. This freedom manifests itself in works of "productive genius," works that may be regarded "as the symbol of an individual nature unfolded in the mind—as evidence of an unoppressed spirit of life in the soul . . ." (qtd. in Klancher 189–90). This soothing language masks the exploitative and repressive actions in which the national genius was daily engaging at home and abroad.

Keats did not share these sentiments; in 1819 he saw the distresses of the day, including government prosecutions for political and religious dissent, as favorable signs for revolutionary change (*Letters* 2: 193–94). It is, then, all the more striking that, however unconsciously, the poetic productions of his annus mirabilis come close to valorizing an ideology of mental power and imaginative production that was forcefully exploited by the apologists for the suppression of labor unrest and for capitalistic expansion in England and its colonies. To think about the ideological implications of Keats's "Ode to a Nightingale" is to ask about its relation to what Foucault calls "the politics of truth" exercised by the systems of power. "Each society has its regime of truth," he explains, "the types of discourse which it accepts and makes function as true" and the means by which it sanctions what counts as truth (131). By obscuring the social specificities of "hungry generations" while foregrounding the desires and failures of the individual imagination, Keats's lyric becomes unwittingly enmeshed in the ideological production of truths that sustained the contemporary social and economic forms of hegemony. But readers can uncover some subtle though not unambiguous ways in which this poetic text questions assumptions such as aesthetic autonomy and clears a space for possible alternatives to the dominant ideology that the poet cannot yet articulate.

THEORETICAL APPROACHES

Teaching Keats from the Standpoint of a Deconstructive Phenomenology

Tilottama Rajan

One of the biggest challenges faced by the teacher of Keats is the deceptively programmatic quality of his career. As early as "I stood tip-toe" he announces the myths around which he does in fact construct his major poems. In "Sleep and Poetry" he charts the path that he will take in the Renaissance pursuit of fame: a progress from pastoral through romance to epic. Related to this essentialist proclamation of a poetic identity that seems to precede any engagement with language is (at least in canonical undergraduate poems such as the odes and romances) a certain formal clarity that makes his texts very different from those of Shelley, with their involuted syntax and labyrinthine narrative structure. The well-wrought quality of the poems appeals to students who want a schematic paradigm of late Romanticism. It also offers a formidable temptation to teachers who feel pressured to be formulaic at the end of the year. But related as it is to a foregrounding of poetic convention and to the archaism of Keats's settings, this artificial neatness also troubles thoughtful students. They find Wordsworth more down-to-earth and Blake, although obscure, more committed to modern concerns. The long tradition of treating Keats as a sceptic or ironist (Stillinger; Sperry; Dickstein) helps to counter this impression. Teaching Keats in courses that stress uncertainty and open-endedness (a Romantic survey and a course on ideas in Romantic literature), I regard my task as twofold: to introduce students to more unsettled poems, like "The Fall of Hyperion," and to present the canonical poems as complicating themselves not at a textural level but rather in the spaces between forms and in the inadequacy of form or myth to content.

More than any other Romantic poet, Keats experimented with a variety of modes and genres: the classical and the romantic (as defined by contemporaries like August and Friedrich Schlegel); the lyrical and the narrative; romance, epic, and myth. The question of form as a mode of awareness is crucial to my approach. It provides a way of considering what is specifically literary in a poem without being drily formalist. It also allows me to deal with the psychological problem of whether poets can achieve identity through their work and yet does not require my seeing identity as something that exists outside language. In a course that alludes to background, one can point out that this "phenomenological" approach to forms was actually a Romantic invention, introduced by Schiller in *Naive and Sentimental Poetry* when he replaced the concept of genre with the more flexible category of mode. Modes, or "moods" (such as the naive and the sentimental themselves), are forms of consciousness that cut across formal distinctions between poetry and drama. They are "adjectives," whereas genres might be thought of as "substantives." Equally important is Hegel, whose *Aesthetics* considers the internal tensions that make it necessary to replace one mode by another and who sees the succession of forms on a world-historical level as a quest in which "Spirit" achieves self-knowledge and identity with itself. Hegel's account of this quest may be too teleological. But if one adapts his approach to the microcosm of the individual oeuvre, it provides a way of seeing an existential connection between disparate forms. Hegel is interested in the inadequacy of form to content, the gap between aesthetic ordering and the thought process underlying it. The only mode in which there is a link between "theme" and "execution"—the classical—is resultingly limited, a cold pastoral. In other words, Hegel's forms are not modes in which the creating consciousness achieves identity with itself so much as modes of representation (with all that that term currently implies).

The question I pursue is that of (self)-representation, whether literary forms can make the self or its ideas fully present to the world. For Keats (unlike Shelley) the problem is not that language, as an equivalent to being in the world, displaces and defers the illusion of a homogeneous set of beliefs. Keats initially associates literature with beauty and literary craft, with form rather than process. Thus his encounter with the problem of difference involves recognizing that language is more complex than form, that received forms prematurely impose a shape on a subject that has not achieved identity with himself. My concern with "difference" is obviously deconstructive. But my approach is a phenomenological deconstruction, concerned with difference in psychological rather than tropological terms. Although I have learned enormously from the work of Derrida and de Man, I do not make unqualified use of it in teaching at any level or in my own writing. Yale poststructuralism may be too abstruse for many pedagogical purposes. But here that abstruseness arises because poststructuralism is not quite true to a period in which the notion of a consciousness or self remains central, if problematic. These theoretical labels, of course, are not ones that I use in class. What I do say is that a sensitivity to difference goes hand in hand with the Romantic shift from finished products to processes (whether historical or psychological). Correspondingly, when we talk about that crucial term *imagination*, we must treat it not just as a substantive but also as a process.

I have begun with speculations I actually interweave into a number of classes that start with close readings. Initially, I approach Keats by discussing the development that occurs through three crucial letters. The letter on the imagination as Adam's dream (*Letters* 1: 185) introduces the theme of imagination as a gateway to a paradise in which reality is the completion of desire. The transformation of vision into truth is instantaneous, a simple matter of awakening, because existence in time is absent from this letter. The entry of time and therefore difference in the letter on life as a mansion of many apartments (*Letters* 2: 280–82) greatly complicates matters. Crossing the threshold from the infant chamber into the chamber of sexual and intellectual awareness, Keats encounters dark passages instead of a dream that comes true. The letter hovers between a sense of blockage and a teleological faith in a shadowy third chamber that will make the fall into self-consciousness a fortunate one. Finally, in the letter on life as a vale of soul making (*Letters* 2: 100–04), he renounces the idea of perfectibility and the notion that imagination can create a paradisal climate for itself in a world that has seasons. But he sees the dark passages in (mental) life as constitutive of an identity that is still in process.

The story I tell is of the development of Keats's imagination from hedonistic to sceptical. In part, I tell it by discussing the modes of functioning of various poems. Students need thematic contexts for such a discussion. "I stood tip-toe" and "Sleep and Poetry" provide me with pre-texts, as it were. The former introduces Keats's major myths but does so in a series of vignettes or episodic instants whose brevity avoids the underside of these myths that is disclosed when they are given narrative or temporal development. The form of the poem allows me to suggest that by contrast extended narratives are inherently self-complicating. "Sleep and Poetry" rehearses the desired stages of Keats's career and indicates that the aesthetics of pleasure achieved in the pastoral mode can be retained as a higher innocence in the epic world of agony and strife. There is, however, an evasive failure of narrative in that Keats cannot describe this world and loses sight of the chariot. Again, by contrast, this poem lets me introduce the issue of narrative. It prepares the way for the romances and Hyperion poems by suggesting that their narrative form will complicate the poet's ideals and force him to work them out through specific characters and situations.

The major texts are far less conclusive than these youthfully panoptic poems. The received myths and genres put Keats through the equivalent of Lacan's mirror stage: they offer him a public and traditional identity, but this identity proves illusory and simplifyingly rigid, an occasion for self-reflection. In exploring Keats's formal restlessness, the letters again provide a starting point. Significantly, Keats avoids the essay or treatise in presenting his aesthetic speculations. Letters emerge on the boundary between the public and private: what they say is always provisional and situational. Being written to others, letters raise the problem of self-representation as a masking process: the writer identifies with positions that are created partly in reaction to, or in emulation of, the other person and that do not quite express the "self." Letters are also an easily graspable way for the teacher to introduce the intertextuality that is crucial to a poet who works with inherited myths and conventions. For the letter is not the autonomous utterance that the New Critics taught us to see the poem as being, and it can crystallize the ways in which poems too are not autonomous and self-identical. Written in response to another letter or conversation, it repeats this other position as text rather than fact while becoming itself a text open to the scepticism of the reader. Using the intertextuality of the letter as a paradigm, we can see Keats's use of received myths and genres as similarly part of a dialogue with himself and with tradition.

I pursue these concerns of form as mask and of intertextuality through the late romances. Northrop Frye defines romance as a mode in which the hero is superior to us and to circumstances (*Anatomy* 33). Romance, the creation of an ideal otherworld, is also centrally linked to Romanticism, the imaginative overcoming of reality. In "The Eve of St. Agnes" Romanticism becomes a thematic concern as embodied in the triumph of love and, as Earl R. Wasserman has shown, in the transformation of Adam's dream into reality (101–12). In "Isabella," if read naively, romance is inversely celebrated: love is defeated but not uprooted, and the power of Isabella's imagination to transform reality is symbolized in the basil plant, where beauty grows out of horror. But romance is a mask with which Keats is uneasy. The introduction of tellers into these poems raises the question of (mis)representation, of literary convention as a falsification. Presented to us as an antique tale or as the song of a "simple minstrel," romance loses its (author)ity, and the traditions it embodies are set in the space of textuality. Moreover, that these poems are narratives allows discrepancies between "theme" and "execution" to emerge. As the "consequitive reasoning" (*Letters* 1: 185) that links the tableaux in which "The Eve" seeks to arrest time, the narrative process reveals troubling depths in the relationship of the lovers that the poem's pictorialism flattens out. Similar depths in "Isabella" have been analyzed by Stillinger (*Hoodwinking* 31–45) and Rajan (*Dark Interpreter* 103–04, 129–33). Students are always responsive—in view of Keats's romanticizing imagination—to the macabre irony of his decision to symbolize the transplanting of love into memory through an actual plant, as if symbolic and literal reading, romance and realism, are being played off against each other. Finally there is the archaism of the poems, which dislocates us from our own time without allowing us to feel at home in the past. This double displacement is crucial not only to these texts but, more generally, to the hermeneutic encounter between readers and texts. Similar displacements and ironies contribute to the indeterminacy of "Lamia," a different kind of antiromance, which explicitly exposes Lamia as symbol for the romantic imagination's ability to transcend space and time through verbal magic. The psychological complexity of the narrative and the shifting, metamorphic nature of her mythic identity are at odds with the allegorization of Lamia as imagination. Though the plot moves irresistibly toward her exposure, the presence of a narrator once again makes us conscious of plot as convention, unsettling the poem's irony as Keats had earlier unsettled the romanticism of "The Eve."

Lastly, I turn to Keats's epic myths and to "Hyperion" as an introduction to its revisionary successor. In the course that includes background, I will have already discussed the increasingly anthropological treatment of myth by philosophers like F. W. J. Schelling, reflected in Blake's statement, "All deities reside in the human breast." If we think of the gods as projections of human faculties, it is easier to see that "Hyperion" is really about the attempt to achieve poetic identity through a struggle between dejection and creativity, a conflict given world-historical consequences through the myth of the Titans and the Olympians. Saturn experiences a loss of creativity, and Apollo is meant to go through the development from lyric to epic described in "Sleep and Poetry." My discussion focuses on gaps between theme and execution. The theme of the imagination as divine (introduced in "Ode to Psyche") is at odds with the way the poem dwells on the death of the gods. The received Miltonic and epic pattern of encyclopedic history, in which the fall into self-consciousness is redeemed in the grand march of time, is belied by the inability to provide more than a fragment of the epic. Hence the desired resolution to Keats's creative problem (how the poet can be a god in a world that includes the fall of empires and the death of individuals) can only be projected abstractly and appears as a mask that Keats cannot wear, a Miltonic style in which his own voice cannot find a home. Most important is the poem's failure as narrative: its paralyzed existence as a series of sculptural tableaux that Keats is unable to link in a forward movement.

Epic is a mode of poetic identity that claims absolute authority based on global vision. "The Fall of Hyperion" is manifestly not an epic, being Keats's version of Yeats's "Circus Animals' Desertion," in which he lets his ladder down into his heart to analyze the motives underlying the poet's self-projections. Indeed, where "Hyperion" presented itself as an epic fragment in search of wholeness, "The Fall" further dismembers its precursor and replays only shards and relics of the fragment. Because of this final poem's complexity, my discussion tends to be directed toward thematic commentary, which has its problems when one is using a deconstructive approach. The poem begins with an abrupt transition from a paradise that offers the poet the temptation of immortality to an ancient Greek sanctuary whose story is that even the gods are mortal. The forlorn scene that is the site of the poet's awakening in poems like "Ode to a Nightingale" and "La Belle Dame sans Merci" is, however, in this poem, a sanctuary invested with value. I sometimes relate this opening contrast of settings to a discussion in Nietzsche: *The Birth of Tragedy* uses the Olympians and their complicating link to the Titans as a way of rejecting the Christian religion, which either claims perfectibility or laments its absence by dismissing life as a vale of tears, in favor of a Greek religion that is protoexistentialist. I emphasize the existential character of the poem and its consequent decoupling of poetry from the idealistic forms of epic, romance, and myth. The story of the gods (no longer epic but tragic) is seen inside the head of Moneta, who, as Muse, is a phantasm in Keats's own mind. I therefore stress that the poem has the quality of a psychoanalytic encounter, in which identity must emerge (if at all) through a process that discloses the gaps in the poet's self-representation.

One of my major concerns is with how Keats, for the first time, experiences writing as language rather than form. Theme does not precede execution in "The Fall": the poem exists not as a mental construct that is complicated by its embodiment in language but simply as the process of its own writing. Significantly the poem has no genre in the traditional sense, except as a fragment. Part dialogue and part visionary theater, it deconstructs the idea of monologic metastatement and abandons the epic claim of "Hyperion" to understand the grounds of things in favor of a dramatistic presentation in which the emphasis is not on plot and causality (on drama as mimesis) but rather on the spectator (on drama as ritual experience). Correspondingly there is a shift of focus from the emphasis in "Hyperion" on the events the poet sees to the process of vision itself and to content as an effect of this process. For readers this means that thematic summaries of the content are at variance with the poem's mode of functioning. I find it more practical, however, to propose such summaries and situate them than to abandon them altogether. To correct the arrogance of thematic abstraction, I give considerable attention to the initial dialogue between Keats and Moneta and to the way attempts to define the poet and separate him from the dreamer are constantly frustrated in the course of being articulated. At first the slipperiness of language is dizzying for the speaker, who can be sure neither that he is a poet nor that he is not. But the speaker's failure to achieve identity, in the sense of something public and fixed, is the site of the self's emergence as well as its deconstruction. For if he is not a poet he also does not seem to be a dreamer, and this chameleonlike capability liberates him to write (1.302–08) and marks his difference from those statuesque gods who have achieved identity only in death. What he writes is a "half-unravell'd web" in which unraveling (revealing) the truth about the gods is also unraveling (untying) the text of truth. In a poem that is after all a fragment, a ghost sonata inhabited by shades and statues whom we never know from the inside, our attempts at thematic interpretation are necessarily also "unravelings."

Keats's "Gordian Complication" of Women

Susan J. Wolfson

Teaching Keats in relation to his attitudes toward women is a specialized
approach with several pedagogical values. One is the range of literary and
social figures brought into prominence through a reading of poems, letters,
and biographical material. These texts illuminate a crucial characteristic of
Keats's imagination: more than any of the other male Romantics (except
perhaps Shelley), Keats tends to represent ecstatic or visionary experience
as an encounter with a female or feminized figure; correspondingly, his
deepest anxieties take shape in confrontations with power in a female form
or in separations from, losses of, or betrayals by women. Lastly, because
these circumstances play into certain recognizable cultural ideologies of gender, the issues of feminist criticism help us appreciate the literary and social
contexts within which Keats wrote and attempted to make a name for himself.

In a survey course, this approach may be focused on a few well-known
odes and romances; in more specialized or advanced courses, it may be
extended and elaborated across the canon. While my discussion draws on a
range of Keats's writings, it is possible to discover the interest of its terms
even treating only a few poems. Using an efficient lecture or directed discussion, one can begin a consideration of Keats's representations of the
feminine with a focused survey of the field. Students will recall how in the
early poems various wish-fulfilling adventures of the adolescent male imagination converge on sensuous goddesses and nymphs or how the larger plot
of *Endymion* conflates quest romance with erotic luxury. Some may remem-
ber that in the crucial post-*Endymion* sonnet on *King Lear*, Romance itself
is figured as a woman—a figure, moreover, antithetical to the literary tradition Keats's poet hopes to join. Most students will be able to comment on
the peculiarities of romantic love in the three tales for which the 1820 volume
is named, *Lamia, Isabella, The Eve of St. Agnes, and Other Poems*. And
they may realize that even if the Great Odes do not engender such plots,
their central figures are gendered as feminine: Psyche is a goddess absorbed
into the mind; the nightingale's enchantment is a "fancy" that "cannot cheat
so well / As *she* is fam'd to do" (emphasis added); the Grecian urn not only
is greeted as an "unravish'd bride" but doubles the unsettling implications
of this term in its several displays of female figures about to be ravished—
the "maidens loth" pursued by "men or gods," the fair maid pursued by the
"Bold lover," the "heifer" with "all her silken flanks with garlands drest" for
ritual sacrifice. In "Ode on Indolence"—a mood Keats calls "a state of ef-
feminacy" (*Letters* 2: 78)—male desire turns ambivalently on three female
figures (Love, Ambition, and Poesy); Melancholy is a goddess who perplexes
"Beauty" and death; Autumn repeats this perplexity in vaguely feminine
form—perhaps an androgyny of the male reaper and the feminine Ceres,

the agent of his bounty. In the Hyperion fragments, Keats variously casts tutelary goddesses, Mnemosyne and Moneta, in roles crucial to the career of the hero. And his last lyrics express the agitations of self-definition in his romance with Fanny Brawne. Even if not exhaustive, any survey will reveal how the matrix of feminine figures in Keats's literary imaginings makes his a version of English Romanticism that intersects provocatively with the politics and poetics of gender.

With these points of attention, I ask students to think through the material in more detail. What do the categories of gender suggest or signify to Keats? Which relationships between men and women seem most compelling to him? Which most disturbing? What balances of power seem at issue? When does he admire or sympathize with women, or a woman, and in what terms? When does hostility appear? What occasions perplex? Which poetic figures seem most involved with Keats's anxieties? When and how do Keats's poetic strategies suppress or contain his anxieties? Which plots or figures seem compensatory? Which evasive? While there are not yet many critical studies treating these topics, good resources are Dorothy Van Ghent's *Keats: The Myth of the Hero*, which details the mythic figures and tales informing Keats's (and other Romantics') stories of young men's encounters with female figures; Leon Waldoff's *Keats and the Silent Work of Imagination*, a lucid psychoanalytic treatment of Keats's ambivalence about women; Theresa M. Kelley's "Poetics and the Politics of Reception: Keats's 'La Belle Dame sans Merci,' " a probing study of how Keats implicates the otherness of the feminine in the otherness of allegory; Margaret Homans's "Keats Reading Women, Women Reading Keats," which queries the ideological issues in Keats's treatment of women as texts and as readers; my article, "Composition and 'Unrest,' " on the vexed formal dynamics of Keats's late lyrics of desire for Fanny Brawne; and my essay "Feminizing Keats" on the way Keats's poetics of gender affected his reputation and critical reception. Also valuable is *Romanticism and Feminism*, a collection of essays edited by Anne K. Mellor, with much suggestive commentary on Keats, particularly by Karen Swann and Sonia Hofkosh. For exploring these issues, the most helpful edition of the poems is that of Miriam Allott, who provides a wealth of notes on literary echoes and literary and mythological sources as well as the references to revealing passages in the letters.

This approach has adversarial potential, for it inevitably discovers Keats's sometimes unpleasant judgments about women. Although such attitudes may be read in many of Keats's contemporaries, their appearance in Keats may distress students for whom he is a favorite—the most sympathetic of the Romantics, most readily valued for moral and intellectual flexibility. Some students may even resent a discussion that threatens their admiration for Keats and his poetry. It is important to explore these disturbances and the tensions evoked between moral critique and imaginative attraction (itself a Romantic issue)—even if the result complicates previous understanding. Other students, of course, may bristle at the sexism in much of Keats's poetic and epistolary discourse; there is no avoiding it: "the generallity of women," Keats says, "appear . . . children to whom I would rather give a Sugar Plum than my time" (*Letters* 1: 404); the "inadequacy" of "Women with few exceptions" is that they "are equally smokeable"—that is, so easily read as to be vulnerable to ridicule (2: 19); at best, he pays a dubious tribute to their supposed innocence: "Women must want imagination and they may thank God . . . that a delicate being can feel happy without any sense of crime" (1: 293). He tends to admire women chiefly, sometimes exclusively, in terms of physical charm: replying to Fanny Brawne's "half complaint once" that he seemed to love only her "Beauty" (2: 275), Keats protests that without "your Beauty . . . I could never have lov'd you—I cannot conceive any beginning of such love as I have for you but Beauty. . . . So let me speak of you [sic] Beauty" (2: 127). Some readers may prefer to see this as aesthetic idealism, but when the poet of "Ode on Melancholy" urges men to view, and control, women's anger as an aesthetic prospect—"if thy mistress some rich anger shows, / Emprison her soft hand, and let her rave, / And feed deep, deep upon her peerless eyes"—we can see how this prescription rejects the woman's subjectivity, restricts her expressiveness, and forcefully appropriates her as a resource of rich nurture for the artist or artful lover. The obverse of this aesthetic is, in fact, a contempt for women who are less appealing to the male gaze. Keats insists that he will not spend "any time with Ladies unless they are handsome" (2: 20); after copying out at length an appallingly misogynist diatribe from Burton's *Anatomy of Melancholy* that details all "such errors or imperfections of boddy or mind" the admiring lover will overlook in his mistress, Keats remarks to George and Georgiana, "There's a dose for you—fine!! I would give my favou[r]ite leg to have written this as a speech in a Play: with what effect could [the right actor] pop-gun it at the pit!" (2: 191–92).[1] How should we assess the trade Keats proposes —a favorite leg in exchange for the effective verbal weapon against female physical allure?

If Keats's views of women trouble some students' views of Keats, it helps to remind them that Keats himself is acutely aware of not having "a right feeling towards Women," of harboring what he describes to Benjamin Bailey as "a gordian complication of feelings, which must take time to unravell" and "care to keep unravelled." He knows he "could say a good deal about this" (*Letters* 1: 341–42), and threads of this complication weave through letters and poems. I urge students inclined to prosecute Keats for not being as good a friend to woman as he is to man not to deny their judgments but to incorporate them into a more subtle understanding. Keats's preoccupation with women's appearance and his aggression toward them emerge from a deep anxiety about how women perceive his longings: "I do think better of Womankind than to suppose they care whether Mister John Keats five feet hight likes them or not" (*Letters* 1: 342; cf. 2: 61 and 2: 275). We can show students how often Keats's representations of women engage figures of male vulnerability. "Ode on Melancholy," for instance, works a stunning reversal on the male poet's restraint and appropriation of his mistress's anger, his intent to "feed deep, deep upon her peerless eyes": by the poem's close, it is a "She," "Veil'd Melancholy," who has power and he who is appropriated and desubstantialized: "His soul shall taste the sadness of her might, / And be among her cloudy trophies hung." And we can see how deeply these figures of entrapment and dissolution inform the letters to Fanny Brawne: "Ask yourself my love whether you are not very cruel to have so entrammelled me, so destroyed my freedom" (2: 123). Keats's transformation of his felt powerlessness into her power is clear enough, and his ambivalence about the pleasures of such surrender intensifies over the summer of 1819: "it seems to me that a few more moments thought of you would uncrystallize and dissolve me—I must not give way to it—but turn to my writing again —if I fail I shall die hard—O my love, your lips are growing sweet again to my fancy—I must forget them—Ever your affectionate Keats—" (2: 142).

While the issue of Keats and women cannot be treated comprehensively in one or two classroom sessions, "La Belle Dame sans Merci" affords a productive preliminary focus—not only because it succinctly dramatizes an ambivalent reading of an intriguingly ambiguous woman but also because its complexity offers suggestive points of departure to related circumstances in other poems, letters, and biography. Students will observe a contradiction in the two impressions given by the poem's title: the beauty of the woman and the treachery of her attribute (or, rather, deficiency). They will also note the many contrasts between the knight's tale and his present appearance: if he is pale, "haggard," and ailing, she was "Full beautiful"; if he loiters in "anguish" and "fever," she was light-footed and "wild." She seemed to "sing / A fairy's song," but now "no birds sing"; he was sure "she said— / I love thee true" and "look'd at me as she did love," but he is now "woe-begone." Where there were flowers enough for him to make "a garland for her head, / And bracelets too, and fragrant zone," now the "sedge is wither'd from the lake"; where she offered nurture—"roots of relish sweet, / And honey wild, and manna dew"—and "lulled [him] asleep" in "her elfin grot," he dreamed of starvation and awoke alone, withering "On the cold hill's side."

This dream seems to hold a solution to the mystery of these reversals: "pale kings, and princes too, / Pale warriors" announce in concert, "La belle dame sans merci / Hath thee in thrall!"—their "starv'd lips" seeming to prefigure the knight's present depletion, their "horrid warning" glossing his present state. Indeed, the knight himself grants these voices undisputed interpretive authority: "And this is why I sojourn here," he answers his questioner. Because this "why" is privileged in the title of the poem, students may want to conclude that the erstwhile "beautiful" lady was actually treacherous and deceptive. For support they may cite earlier versions of this figure in Keats's poetry—Circe, the cruel enchantress Endymion hears about from Glaucus; the "Fair plumed syren," Romance, in the sonnet on reading *King Lear* (as well as an infamous inventory of femmes fatales in literary tradition). And they may look forward to Lamia's concealed identity as a snake (elaborated by Keats's conscious echo of various Satanic seemings in *Paradise Lost*) or the suspicions of infidelity that surround the figure of "Fanny" in late lyrics and contemporaneous letters. Yet the knight's account in "La Belle Dame" contains several logical perplexities and lacunae that the students can ponder, especially in relation to anxieties Keats expresses in other poems and letters. For one, the knight is not simply a powerless thrall. No sooner does he meet this lady than he courts her, claims possession of her ("I set her on my pacing steed"), and translates her words into terms that satisfy his own desire: "And sure in language strange she said— / I love thee true." If students wonder (rightly) what authorizes so sure an interpretation, we can point out that Keats reproduces the problem for us with the ambiguous syntax of the knight's earlier phrase, "She look'd at me as she did love." Does *as* denote simultaneous action, her unity of feeling and gesture? Or does it reveal his act of surmise, *as if*? If students want to use that suggestion of error to confirm the revelation of the dream, we can show them how the identity of the lady eludes exact definition: it is difficult to point to any action of hers, beyond her disappearance, that can be construed as cruel or enslaving. There is, moreover, the odd and unexplained detail that she herself seems in the thrall of some unnamed grief: "she wept, and sigh'd full sore," the Knight remembers.

The very confusion of these statements and their ambiguous significance mark the degree to which Keats has figured "la belle dame" less as a lady than as a text bound to the rhetoric of the men who interpret her. He makes it necessary to interpret the interpreters, for he has cast them all (knight, kings, princes, warriors) in the patriarchal order—an order whose power and integrity require rejection of the regressive enjoyment the knight associates with the lady, namely, his relapse from quest, battle, conquest, and government into a world of erotic luxury, sensuality, and near infantine pleasure. "La belle dame sans merci" may thus be the name assigned to whatever it is that urges withdrawal from the masculinist ethic and patriarchal duties coded in the poem's other important name, "knight at arms." Might one coordinate this conflict with Keats's general reservations about romance, especially its evasion of the epic themes and epic imperatives imposed by the tradition of male writing to which he aspires? By representing its eponym as a text of problematic interpretation by a community of men and in shifting the terms of evaluation within one particular account, "La Belle Dame" provokes the question with a slipperiness that suggests the psychological stress with which the lady is burdened.

We can read anticipations of such conflicts in earlier poems where nymphs and goddesses inhabit worlds isolated from social responsibilities or on an arc of development preceding adult demands—what Keats foresees in "Sleep and Poetry" as the "strength of manhood" that "must pass" recesses of joy for "a nobler life" of "agonies" and "strife" (163, 123–24), or what, in his famous comparison of life to a "Mansion of Many Apartments," he deems the "grand march of [male] intellect" that begins only when the "Chamber of Maiden Thought" opens out into "dark passages" (*Letters* 1: 280–82). We can remind our students how a critical perspective on erotic retreat writes the deep psychological drama of *Endymion*: if Cynthia is a "completed form of all completeness" (1.606), such totality is also, as Stuart Sperry shows, a form of regression; "lapp'd and lull'd" with her "along the dangerous sky" (1.646), Endymion, as Keats's verbs imply, flirts not only with "distract[ion]" but with the near death of adulthood in a waking life that now seems "weary" (1.653–55, 710). The unmanning of adult responsibility by erotic luxury is not just the narrator's suspicion but a subject of explicit reproof in that voice of busy common sense, Peona. The charm is strained further, as both Sperry and Christopher Ricks help us see, by the spectacle of Venus doting on Adonis and is all but dissolved in Circe's ridicule and treacherous reversals (see Sperry 101–09; Ricks 12–14). Students will notice how the temptation to retreat from the social demands of adult male life gets projected, in this poem and others, as entrapment by the supernatural and the feminine, while the need to punish this impulse (or at least exercise judgment against it) is suggested by the way Keats typically has the male lovers betrayed to a fatally forlorn state.

The undoing of vocation by the feminine not only haunts the erotic dynamics of early poems but persists as an issue throughout Keats's career: we see similar trouble in Lycius's romance with Lamia, where Keats pits erotic fascination, with disastrous consequence, against the claims of "proper" manly life. There is an important variation, however: Lamia is not just a temptation from such summons but is in turn destroyed by that world—as a result of her coercion by Lycius's desire for a traditional display of male power, namely, his insistence on public marriage to flaunt her as his prize. This shift in the characterization of Lamia from the corrupter of male self-sufficiency to the victim of male aggression escalates into outright opposition the ambivalent interpretations of the lady in "La Belle Dame." A possibly Satanic, and certainly manipulative, vamp in part 1, Lamia in part 2 is the pathetic casualty both of Lycius's tyranny ("says K—'Women love to be forced to do a thing, by a fine fellow—*such as this'* " [*Letters* 2: 164]) and of Apollonius's "cruel, perceant" unmasking. That all three are debased or destroyed by such exercises of power may even suggest Keats's provisional criticism of the sexual ideologies he senses in his gordian complication of feelings about women. These complications also occur in "Isabella" and "The Eve of St. Agnes." In the former tale, we may ponder Keats's attraction to the story in Boccaccio in which a secret romance ends with the young man's murder by Isabella's worldly brothers, who deem their interests violated— and in which (moreover) the heroine is peculiarly punished, bereft first of the person and then the remnant on which she dotes. In the latter romance, we may consider how intriguingly undecided Keats's characterization of Madeline is: she appears variously as an innocent dreamer, an object of rapt devotion, a subject of soft ridicule, and a target for appropriative designs, opportunistic manipulation, and, some have argued, calculated betrayal.

All these plots are driven by a tension between the impulse toward self-dissolution activated by erotic desire and the impulse toward self-sufficiency that remains hostile to figures exciting such desire. Students who study these attitudes in Keats's late lyrics will see how the interplay of suspicion, resistance, and devotion that encompasses the beloved brings into revealing coordination Keats's literary and social figurings of the feminine as a force against male independence. This plot also underwrites the images through which Keats represents his vocation. If his "chief poet[s]" and presiders are male (Homer, Shakespeare, Milton, Wordsworth), it is significant that he genders "Poesy" itself as female in his sonnet "On Fame" ("Fame, like a wayward girl"): the feminine is the elusive object of masculine desire— perverse, "coy," enslaving, enchanting, potent, and faithless. It seems no coincidence that when Keats writes that the "Imagination may be compared to Adam's dream—he awoke and found it truth" (*Letters* 1: 185), he uses a simile attributing that ideal to prelapsarian Eden, and, even there, to a dream that deletes the name of the woman who completes, then perverts, that paradise. A clear analogue appears in the way contemporaneous letters and poems represent Fanny Brawne at once as a "dearest love" and a negative muse—an object of deep suspicion and a force against the poet's self-possession.

These female assaults on psychological integrity are explicit in the figures that focus Keats's desire for the material success that will confirm his poetic aspiration. If muses are feminine by tradition, in Keats's writing the assignment of gender to a capacity desired but not securely possessed has more than a conventional charge, for such ascription typically summons that matrix of hostility toward, and fear of, women's power to ratify or reject a young man's petitions for recognition. Such fear is sharply rehearsed in Moneta's challenges to the poet-dreamer of "The Fall of Hyperion," while the power of the marketplace conceived as feminine stimulates resentment and outright hostility in the sonnet "On Fame." Keats bristles at the thought of himself and his writing subject to real as well as figurative feminine favor: he "detest[s]" the prospect of "Women . . . tak[ing] a snack or Luncheon of Literary scraps" (*Letters* 1: 163), and he is adamant about refusing them any power over his own texts. When Richard Woodhouse expresses his concern that certain passages in "The Eve of St. Agnes" might "render the poem unfit for ladies," Keats insists that "he does not want ladies to read his poetry . . . he writes for men" (2: 163), and he deliberately reworks his last stanzas to assail the sentimental taste he associates with women readers—even though he senses the consequences (see 2: 327, the letter to Charles Brown, Aug. 1820). With a striking conflation of women as readers and lovers, he informs his publisher, "I equally dislike the favour of the public with the love of a woman—they are both a cloying treacle to the wings of independence" (2: 144).

Keats's various figures of ambivalence about the power of the feminine evoke his unresolved feelings about his mother. There are two oddly contradictory reports: Joseph Severn recalls Keats's saying that "his greatest misfortune had been that from his infancy he had no mother" (W. Sharp 5n), while Keats's brother George recalls a "doting fondness" for all, "particularly John" (Rollins 1: 314). Not only is this discrepancy extreme, but it bears a peculiar warp in Keats's remark to Severn: his father died years before his mother, yet he seems affected only by maternal absence; moreover, his mother died not in his infancy but a few months into his thirteenth year. Frances Keats's behavior may have inspired her son's radical fiction: she remarried two months after his father's death, then disappeared; when she returned some years later, this formerly lively and passionate woman was alone and consumptive, and she died within two years at a relatively young age. In the interval, young John took charge of her care in acts of compelling intimacy—nursing her, fixing her meals, reading to her, guarding her door as she slept. We can appreciate how such circumstances might perplex the emotions of her teenage son: her doting fondness betrayed by a long and unexplained absence; his relief at her return crossed by angry grievance at her abandonment; her illness perhaps seeming the grim fulfillment of a desire to see her punished; his guilt for his apparently "effective" anger; all this perplexity intensified by her death.

Leon Waldoff shows how Keats's poems and letters split this ambivalence into two kinds of women: one is the "fair maid" who is cherished, protected and who in turn offers joy and security; the other is the woman who betrays the young man's trust, abandons him, or perverts nurture to punishment (see esp. 86–98). At other times such ambivalence appears in opposing attitudes about one woman: the equivocal adjectives that accrue to Romance in the sonnet on *Lear*, for instance, or the conflict between desire and judgment that attaches itself to La Belle Dame and Lamia. Keats suggestively relates these doublings to the era of his mother's disappearance and death: "When I was a Schoolboy I though[t] a fair Woman a pure Goddess, my mind was a soft nest in which some one of them slept though she knew it not." His adult feelings, he realizes, in part redress his sense of betrayal: he cannot "be just" to women "because they fall so far beneath my Boyish imagination" (*Letters* 1: 341). Not only is it remarkable that this boyish ideal still has a hold on the young man, but we may wonder whether the worship of women itself is a psychic defense against, or repudiation of, a hostility denied expression until manhood. Keats's negotiations of the feminine—in his social experience with women, in his epistolary reflections, and in his range of poetic representations—is a complicated and extensive subject. That Keats's writing participates in and elaborates many of the ideological prejudices of his literary and social heritage is undeniable; what makes his particular experience of these issues compelling are the complex acts of imagination they engender.

NOTE

[1]Rollins identifies the passage Keats transcribes as being "from 3.2.4.1 [*Anatomy*, 1806 ed., 2: 314]" and remarks that it is "copied pretty accurately" (2: 191n4).

Keats and the Visual Arts

Nicholas O. Warner

Anyone who has read Ian Jack's *Keats and the Mirror of Art* knows the importance of painting and sculpture to Keats. In teaching Keats's poetry I have found that an interart approach, even if used only to supplement more familiar methods, is immensely rewarding for student and professor alike. To begin with, many students seem to find the rapport between Keats's poetry and works of visual art inherently interesting. Moreover, the use of slides and reproductions provides a welcome change of pace in class and stimulates even the most somnolent of students to take a more active role in class discussions. Above all, an interart approach can deepen our understanding of Keats's poetic imagery and aesthetic philosophy and clarify Keats's ability to absorb artistic influences without being overwhelmed by them.

Teachers using such an approach should, however, be aware of its major drawback—the lack of an agreed-on methodology and vocabulary for describing literary-artistic relations. The instructor can minimize this difficulty by insisting on the need for restraint and tact in discussing visual-verbal parallels and by referring students to responsible, accessible criticism dealing with interdisciplinary approaches to literature and art, such as the works of Jean H. Hagstrum, Wendy Steiner, Chauncey Brewster Tinker, and Ulrich Weisstein.

I organize my teaching of Keats and the visual arts around several key issues, including his highly pictorial imagery, specific influences on his work, affinities between his poetry and the work of various artists, and the iconic element in his verse (poems and passages describing specific works of visual art). Taking into account the interests and level of a particular class, I modify or expand this organization to accommodate other interart topics as well. The interart approach serves not as a substitute for studying Keats's verse but as a tool for enriching that study in the main courses in which I teach Keats—one on the major British Romantic poets and one on literary-artistic relations.

A natural place to begin is with the intensely visual quality of Keats's imagery. First, however, I spend several sessions on Keats's basic themes and stylistic range. I remind students of the theory of *ut pictura poesis*, which has already arisen in our discussions of Blake's composite art and Wordsworth's connections to landscape painting. I describe how important the *ut pictura poesis* tradition was to members of Keats's circle, stressing the interest that figures like Leigh Hunt, William Hazlitt, and Benjamin Robert Haydon took in relations among the sister arts. Noting the obvious visual elements in "Imitation of Spenser," I ask students to select passages from other poems by Keats that seem particularly appropriate for pictorial realization. We discuss what characterizes these passages, such as richness of color, Keats's ability to freeze motion through language, the ways that descriptions of persons or nature suggest portraiture or landscape painting, the interplay of light and shadow, the evocation of actual pictures. In studying "The Eve of St. Agnes," for instance, we explore the ways that Keats's techniques for conveying visual impressions suggest analogies with painting, sculpture, theatrical presentation, and, at times, even film.

Another interart method that clarifies and enriches the experience of Keats's poetry and of his creative processes is to study specific artistic influences on Keats's poetry. To keep this topic manageable, I limit myself to a few striking examples from Jack's immensely helpful book and then discuss Poussin's influence on "Sleep and Poetry," especially on the description of "the realm . . . / of Flora, and old Pan" (101–02). After viewing a few slides of Poussin's mythological and pastoral scenes, my students and I focus on one that had a profound influence on Keats: *The Empire of Flora*. Students are grateful to see what a nebulous character like Flora might look like; more important, they quickly realize the painting's value not merely as a source but as a concrete guide to the kinds of poetry that attracted Keats.

Questions that commonly arise during our discussion include the following: How does a knowledge of the painting's influence on Keats affect our understanding of the poem? How does Keats's description differ from Poussin's painting? Can we detect an implied attitude toward Flora's empire in the painting, and, if so, how does this attitude compare with Keats's?

Similar instances of influence not only clarify later passages in the poem but provide a basis for more detailed examination of Keats's tone, meaning, and style. Toward the end of "Sleep and Poetry" Keats's apparent references to Titian's *Bacchus and Ariadne* and *Diana and Actaeon* often spark spirited arguments about sexual elements in Keats, which lead to an exploration of the "sexualized landscape" in his earlier poetry (Hagstrum, *Romantic Body* 45). In classes where I teach *Endymion*, the discussion of the Titian paintings creates a smooth transition to a consideration of sexuality in that poem. Also helpful are the various paintings of the moon and Endymion by artists like Poussin and Zuccarelli, the ethereal creatures on Wedgwood plaques, and, in contrast, the fleshy, unabashedly sensual youth in Girodet-Trioson's famous painting *The Sleep of Endymion*. Discussion of these works paves the way for such topics as Keats's portrayal of women, for example, in "La Belle Dame sans Merci" and "Lamia."

After looking at specific influences on Keats, we consider the existence of more general affinities (e.g., involving mood, subject matter, the depiction of mythological figures) between his poetry and the paintings and sculptures of Raphael, Titian, Poussin, Claude, Botticelli, and Canova. Jack's volume offers many observations on stylistic and thematic connections between Keats and these artists. I also ask students to consider the validity of analogies proposed by various scholars, such as James Twitchell's comparison of Keats and Cozens, Michael Hinden's comparison of Keats and Vermeer, and Hugh Honour's comparison of Keats and Constable (91). A brief elaboration of Honour's pairing illustrates the pedagogical uses of such analogies.

Probably because thay are already familiar with Constable's art from our earlier study of Wordsworth, my students respond particularly well to Honour's observation that Constable might have said of painting what Keats said of poetry—that it is "a friend / To sooth the cares, and lift the thoughts of man" ("Sleep and Poetry" 246–47). Honour's statement raises an important issue in the study of Keats: the potentially beneficent uses of poetry (and all arts) for humanity. In discussing this idea, we compare the effects that Keats's poems and Constable's pictures have on students—a modest exercise in reader and viewer response that often engenders a freewheeling debate on artistic creation in general and on Keats's particular ideas about the value of the arts, especially poetry. Thus, in addition to its other benefits, the consideration of interart affinities stimulates student involvement in aesthetic and philosophical issues.

An important part of studying Keats's artistic affinities is knowing the kind of art Keats did not admire. Showing students Benjamin West's famous *Death on a Pale Horse*, I have them read Keats's almost equally famous response: "It is a wonderful picture, when West's age is considered; But there is nothing to be intense upon; no women one feels mad to kiss; no face swelling into reality. The excellence of every Art is its intensity . . ." (*Letters* 1: 192). We consider what Keats means by "intensity," how this quality is reflected in his work and that of artists he admired, and how it relates to Hazlitt's notion of "gusto" and to Keats's "pursuit of the sublime" (Watson 141). When time permits, I show some of Raphael's cartoons and Guido Reni's religious paintings and discuss the letter in which Keats deprecates Guido's "mawkishness" and praises the "heroic simplicity and unaffected grandeur" of Raphael's cartoons (*Letters* 2: 19). These comments provide a good introduction to Keats's concern with avoiding sentimentality in poetry and to his quest for "the true voice of feeling" (*Letters* 2: 167). Visual examples of mawkishness are especially helpful to those non-literature majors who consider most Romantic poems "sappy." The contrast between Guido's facile, exaggerated gestures and expressions and Raphael's moving but restrained work demonstrates the gulf between sentimentality and the richly varied emotional nuances of Keats's verse. Especially useful is a four-way comparison of the works of Raphael, Guido, Keats, and any of the many sentimental versifiers who have flourished from Keats's day to the present.

From a study of interart affinities we generally move to Keats's "iconic" poems—those centering on a specific "real or imaginary work of art that [the poet] describes or responds to in some other way" (Hagstrum, *Sister*

Arts 18). After noting earlier poems in this tradition (e.g., Dryden's "Medal" and Wordsworth's "Elegiac Stanzas"), I briefly lecture on the significance of the Elgin marbles to Keats and his contemporaries and assign "On Seeing the Elgin Marbles" for the next class. At that time, we discuss the poem in relation to classical sculpture (including the Elgin marbles themselves) and such pictures as Fuseli's *Artist Moved by the Grandeur of Antique Fragments*. This interart exercise gives students a new awareness of Keats's fascination with classical architecture and sculpture and deepens their understanding of Romantic hellenism as it applies to Keats. More broadly, it serves as a corrective to the oversimplified view of Romanticism as a revolt against everything "classical."

Also discussed in this segment of the course are two iconic poems in miniature—Keats's description of Titian's *Bacchus and Ariadne* and *Diana and Actaeon* from "Sleep and Poetry" (lines 334–36 and 372–80)—as well as "On a Leander Which Miss Reynolds, My Kind Friend, Gave Me" and the verse epistle to John Hamilton Reynolds, where Keats describes Claude's *Enchanted Castle* (or, as it is more correctly and frequently identified in art-library slide collections, *Landscape with Psyche and the Palace of Amor*). Concentrating on the epistle to Reynolds, I have students assess the degree to which the poetic description fits the painting. We consider which features of the painting Keats emphasizes and why, how his description introduces a fanciful history of the castle and projects movement onto an essentially static scene, and the ways that Keats uses an artwork not as a model to be faithfully copied in verse but as a springboard for an examination of his own responses, feelings, and attitudes.

We next turn to Keats's Great Odes, which include English poetry's iconic work par excellence, the "Ode on a Grecian Urn." I remind students that the ode first appeared in a journal emphasizing connections among the various arts; as Helen Vendler comments, "It is no accident that both the 'Ode to a Nightingale' and the 'Ode on a Grecian Urn' were first published in *Annals of the Fine Arts*, a journal whose readers would have taken 'Nightingale' to be a poem on the art of music, and 'Urn' to be a poem on bas-relief sculpture" (77). I draw students' attention to the irony of our not knowing what exact work, if any, inspired this ode and enumerate possible visual sources in Keats's mind: portions of the Elgin marbles, Greek vases from antiquity, plaques and imitation Greek vases by Wedgwood, paintings by Claude, and other works discussed by Dwight E. Robinson and, especially, Jack.

That the poem may have no actual artwork as referent intrigues students and makes them realize that, even were an original for Keats's urn to turn up someday, the poem is not really "about" any single work of art. Students reflect on the association between visual and verbal media, the nature of art in general, and art's relation to reality, imagination, and time. Students exposed, even minimally, to the use of slides in class and to discussion of visual-verbal relations are usually better prepared than others to grapple not only with these aesthetic issues but with the ode's network of challenging questions and with its links to other works by Keats. (On specifically sculptural analogies throughout the odes, see Goslee, "Phidian Lore.")

In more advanced courses, I spend time on Keats's relation to concepts of the sublime, the beautiful, and the picturesque. After explaining these terms in the context of literary and art history, I ask students to compare Keats's landscape descriptions with passages from Thomson, Gray, Collins, and Wordsworth and with picturesque landscapes ranging from those of Salvator Rosa to Gainsborough, Constable, and John Crome. Passages suggesting smooth, graceful loveliness—from *Endymion* and "Sleep and Poetry," for example—are viewed in the light of Edmund Burke's comments on the "beautiful" (Adams 311–12). I relate these passages to examples of the beautiful in art, such as the paintings of Raphael and Guido Reni or the fluid, idealized sculptures of Canova. The complex subject of the sublime in Keats lends itself to comparisons with Longinus and Burke and to interart analysis, with examples ranging from ancient sculpture and Michelangelo to James Martin and Turner. The interart study of the sublime has been especially valuable in guiding students through the "large-limb'd visions" of "Hyperion" and "The Fall of Hyperion"; a good place to begin is with Richard Woodhouse's observation that "Hyperion" "is that in poetry which the Elgin and Egyptian Marbles are in Sculpture" (qtd. in Jack, *Keats* 161). Discussion of the sublime ties in with other aspects of Keats's affinities with the visual arts, but in teaching these works I use artistic sources mainly as background material—the specific connections to art in the Hyperion poems operate on levels of such subtlety that they are best left to consideration in graduate courses.

A more unusual interart approach to Keats's poetry involves study of Victorian, Pre-Raphaelite, and other illustrations to his work (many of which are listed by George Ford). Although I originally used this approach only with advanced students, I find that it works well at all levels of undergraduate instruction. Paintings of scenes from "Isabella" by William Holman Hunt and John Everett Millais, from "The Eve of St. Agnes" by Hunt, Millais, and Arthur Hughes, or from *Endymion* by G. F. Watts often produce strong reactions in students. Responses usually fall into three categories: the paintings are admirable visual renditions of Keats's verse; the paintings are insipid examples of kitsch; the paintings are somewhere in the middle, neither good nor bad. Topics discussed include the nature of Keats's medievalism compared with that of the Pre-Raphaelites, the ways that the later paintings may have shaped readers' responses to Keats, and the depiction of women and sexuality in Keats's poetry and in Pre-Raphaelite art.

Illustrations can also facilitate close examination of textual detail in a single poem. With "La Belle Dame sans Merci," for example, I often use two paintings, one by John William Waterhouse and the other by Frank Cadogan Cowper, both named after Keats's poem. After we study the poem, I show slides of the two pictures and ask students which they prefer as an illustration and why. While such an approach may tempt students to indulge in vague impressionistic comments, one can steer them toward the specifics in both text and illustration. Students seem genuinely challenged when told they must support the claim that, say, Waterhouse's "Belle Dame" is more ambiguous or fairylike than Cowper's and hence more like the woman in Keats's poem; or that one painting is superior to the other as art but inferior as illustration; or that Cowper's impassive blonde captures La Belle Dame's supposed callousness; or that the composition of Waterhouse's figures suggests La Belle Dame's vulnerability in a way that Cowper's does not. Soon, it becomes evident that students' reactions to the illustrations depend on their interpretations of the poem; discussion tests and refines those interpretations by sending students back to the text. Sometimes these exercises result in uncomfortable stretches of silence while students peruse poem or painting, but the silences are worth the quality of commentary they eventually produce.

About midway through my teaching of Keats, I often assign a brief paper asking students to do three things: to select a passage of Keats's verse they would like to have illustrated by any painter of their choice, from any nation or period; to select any painting or sculpture that they wish could be described by Keats; and to explain the rationale for their choices in detailed discussions of Keats's poetry. In general, I find it most useful to assign brief interart exercises during the course of the semester and to use interart topics only as options on term papers and exams. Such topics, although demanding, tend to stimulate students and to generate the kind of liveliness in writing that is also evident in class discussions of literary-artistic relations.

There are many paths other than those outlined here that one could pursue in teaching Keats and the visual arts. A number of poems that I have not mentioned would richly repay interdisciplinary teaching. Or one could focus on a single aspect of Keats's relation to art, such as pictorial details in the odes, or Keats and medieval art, or some Keatsian theme frequently treated by artists, like music, the sea, death, love. But all such variations on the interart approach share one significant value—that of helping students experience more fully the diversity and power of Keats's visual imagination.

Writing on "Isabella" from the Perspective of Composition Theory

Louise Z. Smith

Whoever teaches a Major Author implicitly rejects as premature Roland Barthes's announcement of the "death of the Author" (*Image* 146) but may nevertheless secretly share his objections to "ownership" of texts. The author industry, the enormous edifice of scholarship and criticism (parodied in Frederick Crews's *Pooh Perplex* and Charles Kaplan's *Overwrought Urn*), often overshadows readers' enjoyment of the poetry itself. Instead students ask, "What am I supposed to know about Keats? Which poems am I supposed to value and why? Whose critical views are worth repeating?" They then construct their Keats kits, prefab replicas of the edifice that, they surmise, will enable them to "own" the Author and collect interest (credits, jobs, whatever status "cultural literacy" confers) on their investment of time in reading Great Poems. A poem like "Isabella; or, The Pot of Basil," stamped "Grade D—not for human consumption," attracts diehard antiquarians (if the teacher suppresses the label) but few savvy investors.

Whatever the poem, writing about it seems to be a great trial to the spirit. Students more often ask us, "*What* should I write?"—meaning "What should I demonstrate that I know?"—than they do "*Why* should I write?" Everybody knows why students write papers: to show they have done homework. In literature, and in many other fields, writing tests a student's facility in demonstrating a thesis through various means: (1) by inspecting a work closely (perhaps incorporating experts' readings)—but not so closely as to prevent gerrymandering of evidence that might disrupt the essay's coherence; (2) by repackaging through transcribing the teacher's and other professionals' readings or through piggybacking with previously unimagined or unimaginable combinations (author as crypto-proto-feminist); or (3) by demolishing all previous critical views for failing to notice an as-yet unturned screw in the parts department of the author's oeuvre, biography, reception, and so on. Writing that demonstrates theses to prove ownership of an author's text rarely gauges or engages the writer's enjoyment of what Barthes calls the *scriptible* (writable) text (*S/Z* 10), the text that—instead of revealing itself immediately to the reader as a *lisible* (readable) text would—invites readers to speculate about its potential readings.

Many of the same teachers who revel in a literary text's gaps and undecidables inexplicably continue to penalize students' texts for speculative rambling and to reward them for presenting coherent, complete proofs. Yet in the long run, the *scriptible* text's self-contradiction and indeterminacy are often what make it rereadable. They entice student readers to become lifelong readers. Essays of proof do have their roles, but we too often overlook the value of more exploratory, more meditative ways of writing about literature. Intimations of the author's mortality, then, valuably prompt readers and writers to reexamine the author's canon vis-à-vis its *scriptible* texts. The answer to the query "Why should I write?" might be "To enjoy reading."

Among the questions composition theorists ask, three are most useful to this reexamination: How do we make meaning? What is the nature of error? What is revision? We make meaning, as Ann Berthoff explains, by *gathering* our "chaos" (all the materials through which we might want to think about a subject), generously *listing* observations (and hushing the inner editor that whispers, "That's not relevant" or "This won't pan out"), *clustering* related items (adding whatever new items or observations occur as we do this), *naming* the resemblances among them (their classes, situations, or purposes), and *forming concepts* by relating—perhaps through the use of aids such as double-entry lists, diagrams, and sentence paradigms like "How does who do what and why?"—some of the terms named (46–112). These operations take place not in a linear sequence but dialogically and recursively. We converse back and forth with our writing and reading, asking, "What do I notice?" "How might my observations be related?" "What speculations does this text open to me?" and "What is the lively center of my reading?"

As for the nature of error, composition theory now recognizes that what was once the target of search-and-destroy missions is a valuable window into a writer's mind. As David Bartholomae argues, an error can provide clues about what hypotheses a writer might have formed (about a feature of language) and why. This more positive view of error credits the writer with having made intelligent (though possibly misinformed) choices and having taken risks. Composition teaching then becomes less a matter of eradicating individual errors, more a process of helping students systematically refine their hypotheses. Applied to literature teaching, this attitude encourages readers to speculate why Keats might have chosen, for instance, an abrupt tonal change or a surprising modification of a source. Instead of simply labeling the surprises "flaws" (Ridley 18–56), readers prolong their observations and interpretations of artistic choices while postponing judgment. This approach naturally occasions writing: readers might write to investigate particular discontinuities in "Isabella," to imagine why Keats might have chosen to leave them unresolved, to decide how well his choice worked, or to see how the poem might affect our understanding of Romantic irony.

Revision, says composition theory, is conceptual reconstruction, not cosmetic tinkering. Of course, textual collation provides one view of conceptual change. But beyond that, just as art re-presents experience (that is, makes the past again present in a reader's consciousness), so study of re-visions enables a reader to view a double reflection, that of the author's past in the author's present and that of the author's present in the reader's present.

That double reflection accentuates the ideological differences between the author's and reader's presents (McGann, *Beauty* 5–10). Detection, evaluation, and enjoyment of these differences answers the question Why read? Meditation on them answers the question Why write? Readers can write about an author's poem, asking, How does it make meaning? What authorial assumptions, choices and risks are evident? and How did the author revise and why?

Composition theory will, however, disappoint two other possible expectations. Despite its now clichéd emphasis on writing as process, it will not characterize Romantic poetry as the equally clichéd poetry of process, for process pervades all writing. And despite its efforts to help writers use their own voices, it will leave the "poetry of encounter" (Barth 127) to the psychologically oriented reader-response theorists.

How then can composition theory help us teach "Isabella"? First, it will answer the question, Why teach it?: because unlike Keats's more famous poems, this poem affords students relative freedom from received opinion, freedom to exercise their own powers of observation and judgment. They write often and briefly, not just after but while reading, not just in one-shot formal essays but in daily reading journals, ten-minute mid-lecture or mid-discussion meditations, and several short essays some of which might wind up in longer, more formal pieces of writing. In these frequent writings, students question the author's text more or less as they would one another's essays-in-progress in writing workshops: by looking at connections, choices, risks, re-visions. They share their written, nonevaluative observations: written, to glean many views (not just those of the teacher and a few vocal students); nonevaluative, to encourage exact observations rather than facile generalities (Ponsot and Deen 50–53). The grounds for evaluation (the names for critical standards) emerge dialogically with the back-and-forth movement of composing and revising, observing and speculating, reading and writing.

Readers tell, in their "stories of reading," of many kinds of discontinuities in "Isabella." Instead of dismissing these as authorial errors, they seek explanations. Why might Keats choose a verse form (ottava rima) that concludes with a "point" expressed by the "snap" *cc* rhyme, then leave so many stanzas open? Why constantly juxtapose beauty and horror? Why make the narrator's tone comically inappropriate (he exclaims, when Isabella disinters Lorenzo's corpse, "Ah! wherefore all this wormy circumstance?" [385]) and ironically distanced from romance conventions (he warns readers against wasting tears on the lovers' sorrows [st. 12–13], then, though choosing to render this grisly tale quite graphically, he longs for "the gentleness of old Romance" [387])? Why put him on a soapbox (of Isabella's greedy brothers he asks, "Why were they proud? again we ask aloud, / Why in the name of Glory were they proud?" [127–28]—a snap *cc* rhyme if there ever was one)? Why the many conceptual re-visions of Boccaccio's tale: postponement of details about Isabella's family so that the poem can begin directly with the love idyll (st. 1–11), indictment of the brothers' capitalistic greed (st. 14–18), and others?

The teacher's role is not to suggest reasons for these choices, for to do so would interfere with the students' processes of constructing meanings. Instead, the teacher keeps asking, "Why do you think that?"—promoting further dialogue with the text and helping readers name explicitly their grounds of interpretation. For instance, the students may offer several explanations for Keats's interest in the brothers' greed: Keats may be making Boccaccio's old tale interesting to nineteenth-century readers, criticizing capitalism, revealing the materialism that always underlies idealistic romance, adapting romance conventions to a more realistic setting, questioning the possibility of writing romance in the modern age, or fashioning a new kind of irony. By naming these critical stances, students can see how and to what extent philological, Marxist, and formal analyses complement one another. For the lifelong readers we hope they will become, such an awareness of how they read and why their rereadings create multifaceted and changing truths about a text will be more important—and more enjoyable —than the memory of the interpretations they heard about and transcribed in a course long ago.

If "Lamia" is paired with "Isabella," further observations about "Isabella" will emerge. The verse form of "Lamia" (heroic couplets) moves the story along with a "quick, college-cheer movement" that catches "the gusto of Dryden" (Perkins, "Lamia" 145–46), instead of promising but withholding points as the ottava rima of "Isabella" seems to do. Despite the poem's long history of interpretation generated by the digression on "philosophy" (2.229–38), the narrator of "Lamia" comments fairly unobtrusively compared with the narrator of "Isabella." "Lamia" has one structural division (between the Hermes episode and the story of Lycius) that may be bridged in a number of ways, whereas "Isabella" dances between the original romance and Keats's elaborations. "Lamia" follows Burton rather consistently, whereas "Isabella" constantly challenges its source—tonally, formally, thematically. In short, students are likely to observe in "Lamia" far more formal unity and thematic synthesis, in "Isabella" far more formal and thematic discontinuity, or more positively, dialectic. Should these romances, written within scarcely more than a year ("Isabella" February–April 1818, "Lamia" July–August 1819, with "The Eve of St. Agnes" intervening in January 1819), be considered the creations of a radically discontinuous poetic ability (or sensibility), or should their differences be attributed to experimentation? However readers account for the dissimilarities, their writing on the less canonical work vastly expands their scope for speculation—for naming the poems' characteristics and variously combining those names to make meanings, perhaps using

Berthoff's sentence paradigm, "*How do* narrative comments *do what* to the romance conventions *and why?*"

For instance, critically sophisticated readers comparing "Isabella" with "Lamia" can try to discriminate—to name—different kinds of Romantic irony. We could say that traditional irony depends on the narrator's and reader's acceptance of a knowable, stable hierarchy of value, which the narrator evaluates skeptically, conveying to readers a definite conclusion about the ideal and the actual. But Romantic irony depends on a more tentative exploration of a less knowable flux of value, which the narrator treats with uncertainty (rather than skepticism), conveying illusions that give way to other illusions from which readers conclude nothing (Furst, *Fictions* 229–30). Both poems fit Romantic irony, but "Lamia" is closer to traditional irony than "Isabella." "Lamia" reinforces the social hierarchy and shows the impossibility of Lycius's carrying his ideal love into the real world; "Isabella," however, suspends hierarchy as the heroine retreats with her ideal love (after the brothers steal its material token, the basil plant) into a private world, from which myth arises to be celebrated "through all the country" (502) long after her death. We might ask students how they would name these two kinds of Romantic irony. The cognoscenti might say that "Lamia" is more celebratory and "Isabella" more agonistic or that "Lamia" presents Romantic irony while "Isabella" parodies it. Readers of Bakhtin's *Rabelais and His World* (3–18) might name the irony in "Lamia" "ritualized" and that in "Isabella" "carnivalized." They could argue that in "Lamia" one kind of body is transformed into another but in "Isabella" two bodies (Lorenzo's head and the basil plant) are combined in one (grotesque realism often combines two bodies, one human and the other an object); that while the marriage ritual in "Lamia" is nonregenerative, the absence of ritual in "Isabella" suggests a folkloric regeneration tied to the cycles of the seasons, to time and to myth; and that Lamia's disappearance maintains her individuality, while Isabella's transformation into myth makes her common to all. For literary theorists, what we name these kinds of Romantic irony is critical, in both senses. For lifelong readers, though, the process of speculating about naming is what counts.

When students read and write about each author's and one another's works in the same ways, they may ask whether Great Works make an Author or whether an Author's works are inevitably worth more than a Generic's? We can then widen our chaos to include two letters conveying Keats's own estimate of "Isabella" and its chances for public acceptance. He tells Richard Woodhouse (*Letters* 2: 174; 22 Sept. 1819) that "Isabella" is "too smokeable," that is, too vulnerable to ridicule; the reading public accepts "simplicity of knowlege" only after a poet's death, so "[t]here are very few would look to the reality" of the poem. Henceforth, Keats vows to "use more finesse with the Public" and to "write fine things which cannot be laugh'd at in any way"—like "Lamia," which, he tells George and Georgiana Keats, will "take hold of people in some way—give them either pleasant or unpleasant sensation. . . . What they want is a sensation of some sort" (*Letters* 2: 189; 18 Sept. 1819). These two letters can also contextualize the publication history of the *Poems* (1820). Students could ask how the critics' hostility to the *Endymion* volume might have affected Keats's and his publishers' reluctance to offer anything that could be accused of being sentimental, radical, or "weak-sided" (*Letters* 2: 174; 22 Sept. 1819). In this light, what might their decision to include the "smokeable" "Isabella" with the less vulnerable "Lamia" imply about Keats's attitudes toward his readers?

These two letters could also be used to examine Keats's self-image; how he regarded his role as author. Earlier letters express dislike for others' self-assertive dogmatism, praise his own lack of identity for enabling him imaginatively to inhabit other modes of being, and (just before he begins composing "Isabella") affirm that the poet's energies should flow as naturally "as the Leaves to a tree," a notion that implies little regard for popular opinion. His decision, then, to publish "Lamia" and give the public what it seems to want, yet simultaneously to risk offering the more difficult irregularities of "Isabella," may indicate a delicate mid-career turning point at which the desire for public recognition—or at least acceptance—struggles with the need for private integrity.

Widening our chaos still more, we can connect the question of Keats's roles as author with that of the reception of "Isabella": Why was the poem, so admired by Charles Lamb and John Hamilton Reynolds and popular throughout the nineteenth century, so disliked by many modern critics (Bate, *John Keats*; Blackstone; Bush, *Keats*; Stillinger, "Keats and Romance"), ignored by others (Ende; Rzepka), yet thought worth reconsideration by some (Little; Rajan, *Dark Interpreter*; Smith, "Material")? Critics like René Wellek and M. H. Abrams have defined Romanticism as synthetic, but critics like A. O. Lovejoy and Mario Praz have seen it as dialectic (McGann, *Romantic* 13–36). The ups and downs of "Isabella" correspond roughly to pendulum swings between these views. Those seeking organic unity within the poem and consistency in the romance tradition find "Isabella" atypical of Romanticism and romance, and they devalue it. Those seeking sublime irregularity (in the poem's internal discontinuities and its differences from other romances) find "Lamia" pleasingly Romantic but "Isabella" even more so, more challenging and *scriptible*. As composition students know from their own experience, when they name features in a piece of writing, they reveal their critical ideologies: this means that with respect to this other (Smith, "Enigma" 163–71). This experience, then, helps them recognize that although "Isabella" hasn't changed, critics using different definitions of

Romanticism not only have noticed different features of the poem but also have named and valued the same features differently. The poem's reception offers a lesson in the history of critical ideologies and canon formation.

In 1968 I happened to be sitting in the wrong chair when chunks of the Thorpe edition were doled out around our seminar table. The person to my right got *Endymion*, the one on my left "Hyperion," and I got stuck holding the noncanonical basil pot. In those days, Keats scholars seemed already to have "overwrought" all the good urns, and the invention of composition theory had barely begun. But, luckily, my chunk—what I would later call my "chaos"—included the epistle "Dear Reynolds, as last night I lay in bed." Speculating about its *scriptible* term "material sublime" (69), I turned a seemingly impossible seminar report into an article. Today, I would write from a different chaos, including the "romantic historicism of the visual sublime" and "sublime inversion" (Kroeber, "Romantic" 150–55) and the "duplicity" of iconography and "dematerialization" in paintings by Turner and others (Wolf 322). Would I demonstrate a thesis? What might it be? Who would read it? I won't know until I've written. But this I do know: though since 1974 I've published nothing on "Isabella," bidding the poem "Shut up thine olden pages, and be mute," in the early 1990s speculative re-vision promises the challenge and enjoyment that Keats felt on sitting down to read *King Lear* once again.

Re(:)reading Keats

Donald C. Goellnicht

Because of a common misconception that Keats's poetry cannot be separated from his life, many courses begin the study of Keats with a brief biographical survey, often preceded or accompanied by a cultural survey of the period. Such an approach has the virtue of contextualizing the works and thus disabusing students of the New Critical idea that a text is a transcendent, ahistorical artifact, organically whole, enclosed, unified, and conveying a universal meaning. But it also reinforces students' tendency to read the works as autobiographical documents that show the unfolding greatness of Romantic genius grappling with personal problems. The approach fails to acknowledge that any work of art remains incomplete without an audience and that each audience discovers different elements to value or devalue in a given text. The reader-response tack I describe shifts the focus of attention from the author to the reader, viewing the reader as the final partner in the process of textual production and the reader's psyche as the locus where meaning is ultimately made. I use this approach in a full-year (two-semester) course on English Romantic poetry, which devotes four to six weeks to the study of Keats.

This reader-oriented approach proves especially relevant, I believe, in the light of the radical change in views of reading that occurs in the latter half of the eighteenth century. As Jane Tompkins points out, at this time "criticism moves attention away from literature's social and moral effects and toward the psychology of reading, so that the concept of literary response, from being primarily a social and political one, now becomes personal and psychological" (215). Tilottama Rajan, who deals with these changes in far more detail, labels the decentering of meaning from text to reader a victory for psychological, divinatory reading over structural, grammatical reading and traces these ideas to their origins in biblical hermeneutics ("Supplement").

Tompkins's article is useful to students who seek a historical ground on which to base what they may perceive as new ideas about criticism in general and about Romanticism in particular, ideas that shift the focus to them as readers. They will have encountered earlier, in Blake and Wordsworth, as well as in Coleridge's adaptation of German ideas, some intimations of this shift; but my foundation—or launching slip, in Keats's metaphor—for setting these ideas in motion remains Keats's writing, especially his opinions on reading, writing, and the role of the poet. I have students read the following Keats letters: (1) to John Hamilton Reynolds, 19 February 1818 (*Letters* 1: 231–33), on reading as "delicious diligent Indolence" in which the text acts as a "starting post" or stimulant for the reader's own response or "voyage of conception" that results in a journey of self-discovery; (2) to John Taylor, 27

February 1818 (1: 238–39), on axioms in poetry, the first of which states that poetry must be "a fine excess" so as to allow room for readers to discover in it their "own highest thoughts"; (3) to George and Tom Keats, 21 and 27 December 1817 (1: 192), on the contrast between one of Benjamin West's overdetermined paintings and *King Lear*, a contrast hinging on the play's ability to excite "momentous depth of speculation" in the viewer possessed of "Negative Capability"; (4) to George and Georgiana, 31 December 1818 (2: 19), on Italian engravings that, like Shakespeare's work, leave "so much room for [the viewer's] Imagination"; (5) to Benjamin Bailey, 22 November 1817 (1: 184), on "Men of Genius" and "Men of Power" as two distinct types of poets; (6) to Reynolds, 3 February 1818 (1: 223–25), on Wordsworth as a bullying, didactic poet who cannot write "great & unobtrusive" poetry; (7) to Richard Woodhouse, 27 October 1818 (1: 386–87), on the "camelion Poet," who is absent from his work, versus the poet of "the wordsworthian or egotistical sublime," who attempts to force his philosophy on his readers. (For a more detailed explication of the ideas in these letters, see Goellnicht, "Keats on Reading.")

These letters, which are found in a standard text like Perkins's *English Romantic Writers*, not only introduce students to Keats's important correspondence but also demonstrate in detail that contemporary ideas on reader-response or affective stylistics are not as new as they may appear to be. To introduce my students to contemporary theory, I ask them (either as a group or through individual assignments) to read the following pieces in conjunction with our study of Keats's letters: "The Poetics of the Open Work," by Umberto Eco; "The Reading Process: A Phenomenological Approach," by Wolfgang Iser; and "The Poetic Text within the Change of Horizons of Reading," by Hans Robert Jauss. All these theoretical statements reveal striking parallels with Keats's views on the roles of poet and reader.

One question that usually arises at this point—if it has not surfaced at the outset—is simple, but telling: "What do you mean by 'the reader' or 'a reader'?" There are, of course, a variety of answers, which are variously appealing to different students. Those seeking the assurance of historical grounding might be directed to further works on late-eighteenth-century views of reading (e.g., Rajan's article and Jon Klancher's *Making of English Reading Audiences, 1790–1832;* Richard Altick's *English Common Reader* is also a valuable study of audience). These students are usually interested in constructing an "ideal" Romantic reader, one to whom Keats's sources and allusions would have been familiar. For them, a good starting place is Miriam Allott's annotated edition of the poetry. I point out, however, that Romantic literature was not written with a small, highly educated coterie of readers in mind; Keats himself said he did not wish to be "a versifying Pet-lamb" for a closed group (*Letters* 2: 116). With the increase in literacy rates and the democratizing of education in the latter half of the eighteenth century, audiences were larger and more amorphous, although not so highly educated as the traditional audience had been. Thus the sense of a definite contract between author and audience tended to break down, allowing responses to become more personal and varied.

It is also important to stress that, however much we absorb of the Romantic context and theory, we can never become Romantic readers, because we approach any text with modern or postmodern baggage. We certainly cannot read Keats's poems as if we are ignorant of post-Romantic literature and culture. To demonstrate this point, I introduce the concept of intertextuality and emphasize that, while we recognize allusions, sources, and borrowings from earlier texts in Keats's poetry, we also make connections with works that follow his; that is, intertextuality operates in the mind of the reader, who makes connections both backward and forward from the text in question.

It is helpful to mention that Keats, in his comments on reading, does not attempt to prescribe a particular type of reader or a specific audience group (apart from his piqued statement to Woodhouse, concerning the sexual explicitness of "The Eve of St. Agnes," that "he does not want ladies to read his poetry" [*Letters* 2: 163]). In his pragmatics of reading Keats does not posit an "ideal reader" comparable to Michael Riffaterre's "superreader," who juggles multiple perspectives, or to Fish's "informed reader," who is "neither an abstraction, nor an actual living reader, but a hybrid . . . who does everything within his power to make himself informed" (49); nor does Keats attempt to encode an "implied reader" or "postulated reader" from whom the text, demanding to be accepted "on its own terms," elicits specific responses (Booth, *Rhetoric* 137–44). Keats rebels against this type of authorial control; he is, despite his frequent disillusionment with "the Public" (*Letters* 1: 266–67; 2: 144, 146), interested in what Wayne Booth calls "real readers" ("Reply" 701) and Jauss calls "explicit readers"—in our case, the students in the class. One of my prime aims is to free students from the notion of a single type of reader who can cull a determinate meaning from a poem. My approach emerges, ideally, as a subversive pedagogy that encourages students to explore their individual responses to texts. Keats, after all, complained that "few think for themselves" and feared that his "grand democracy" of readers would not materialize (*Letters* 2: 65; 1: 232).

My "subversive pedagogy" immediately introduces the most problematic question to plague reader-response theories, one that critics have debated to no conclusion: How much freedom does the reader have in shaping his or her response, that is, in creating meaning?; or, alternatively, How much does the text shape and control the reader's response? Is the reader reduced simply to decoding what is encoded in the text, thus falling under the author's power? This is far too complex a question for a definitive answer to be given here or in the classroom. Suffice it to say that I do not side with critics like Norman N. Holland and David Bleich, who claim that readers must be completely free to respond in a form of free association or of totally "subjective criticism." Much more productive, I believe, is Iser's dualistic approach, which posits the reader filling in gaps left in the text; the reader thus retains a certain degree of autonomy in completing the work, although the possibilities of interpretation are set by the parameters of the given text. Writing and reading become a cocreative enterprise of author, text, and reader that allows for pluralistic but not infinite readings. This process corresponds to what Keats seems to have in mind when he describes reading as an individual "voyage of conception"—a voyage in which travelers "greet each other at the journey's end"—or when he uses the metaphor of the reader spinning a web founded on the "solid points" of the text (*Letters* 1: 231–32).

Stating that the text sets the parameters for possible interpretations does not, however, require readers to endorse what emerges from the text; if we are concerned with real rather than implied readers, we must be prepared for students who resist what they interpret. In particular, feminist students (of either gender) often object to the depictions of women in Keats's poetry and correspondence. We should not evade these genuine concerns with platitudinous explanations about the status of women "at that time"; this was, after all, an age that managed to accommodate the works of Mary Wollstonecraft and Mary Shelley. Moreover, Keats demonstrates in his letters an intense self-awareness of his conflicting attitudes toward women (see *Letters* 1: 292–93; 1: 341–42; 1: 402–04; 2: 18–20; 2: 266–67; 2: 327–28), although this self-consciousness never enabled him to overcome or eliminate stereotypes in his poetry: pure, angelic virgins like Madeline; hysterical, dependent women like Isabella; women split between the two extremes of supremely unattainable goddess like Cynthia and exotic, weak, pitiable "other" like the Indian Maid; aloof teachers like Moneta and Mnemosyne; destructive temptresses like La Belle Dame or Lamia. I do not mean to imply that Keats's often highly ambivalent heroines can be dismissed in this simple fashion, but I do think it imperative that we as teachers give credence to feminist students who resist being cast as masculinist readers assenting to these portrayals of women. Students interested in pursuing this topic may be directed to Anne Mellor's *Romanticism and Feminism,* which provides valuable insights on the period; to Susan Wolfson's "Feminizing Keats" and her essay in this volume; to Barbara Schapiro's *Romantic Mother;* and to Helen Ellis's "Food, Sex, Death, and the Feminine Principle in Keats's Poetry."

I turn finally to how all these observations might be applied to the poetry. A good starting point, if time permits, is to examine some of Keats's early poems that *were* written with a specific reader in mind: the epistles "To George Felton Mathew," "To My Brother George," and "To Charles Cowden Clarke." Certain questions immediately surface: Can these poems be read in a meaningful fashion without knowing anything about the addressees? To what extent does knowledge of the addressees (available in any of the standard biographies) affect our understanding of the poems? Does the persona's tone or subject matter change from one addressee to the next? These poems can then be compared with later ones written for a general audience.

From these epistles, I move on to a genre more familiar to students and one to which they come with a host of expectations: romance. I begin with "Isabella" because it raises double expectations, as a romance and as a rewriting of Boccaccio's tale. Some students might be assigned Boccaccio's tale to read in conjunction with Keats's; their responses can be compared with those of students not familiar with the original version. The students who read Boccaccio quickly discover that Keats made significant changes and additions that radically affect their understanding of the work. In particular, he breaks the illusion of a closed romantic narrative by addressing Boccaccio directly in the text to apologize for the changes; the discourse thus shifts from narrative romance to authorial irony. A similar break occurs in the author's tirade against the capitalism of Isabella's brothers. How successful are these mixings of discourses? In addition to Jack Stillinger's *Hoodwinking of Madeline* and Stuart M. Sperry's *Keats the Poet* (an invaluable general study), recent works that may be of assistance here and on the romances in general include Patricia Parker's *Inescapable Romance*, Rajan's *Dark Interpreter*, Robert Kern's "Keats and the Problem of Romance," and Beth Lau's "Madeline at Northanger Abbey." All focus on the dialectical struggle between romance and antiromance, on the self-conscious coupling of a faith in imagination with a radical awareness of imagination's fictitiousness. This struggle calls the reader into the dramatic project.

"The Eve of St. Agnes" is another romance that yields excellent results to this type of approach. Here, I focus more closely on the role of the narrator and the various strategies that shape reader response. Marian Cusac does an excellent job of signaling the narrative intrusions, which William Stephenson interprets as the work of a superb "ironic narrator" in control of the material. Michael Ragussis, however, demonstrates how the narrator ultimately loses control of his own narrative strategies ("Narrative Strategies"). The result is a tale carefully crafted until nearly the end, when the text resists narrative closure and presents us instead with an ambiguous situation in which our protagonists may be alive or dead, spiritual or physical, and in which the sense of time and space becomes dislocated—as indicated by the confusion over tenses in the final stanzas. Any conclusions are thus deliberately, I believe, thrown back onto the reader who must build his or her own truth from the possibilities provided and must complete the text for a narrator who is no longer trustworthy.

A similar, but even more problematic, situation arises in "Lamia" and "La

Belle Dame sans Merci," where the reader's sympathies are split in endings
that remain adamantly open. In "Lamia" we find a series of ambiguities: a
pair of lovers who alternate between the roles of cruel abuser and innocent
victim, a "sage" whose "wisdom" brings total destruction, the age-old conflict
between imagination and philosophy, and the larger question of whether
the narrator's sympathies are consistent or shifting. "La Belle Dame" com-
pounds the confusion surrounding the truth of fiction by presenting us with
a protagonist who dreams of reality while absorbed in a world of fantasy.
These issues obsess Keats as an author, but instead of providing facile answers
his poems invite readers to explore these questions on their own voyages of
discovery.

Although Keats's poems offer no easy solutions, "Hyperion" and "The Fall
of Hyperion," as metapoems dealing with the production and reception of
texts, do present us with paradigms of reading: Apollo in "Hyperion" and
the Poet in "The Fall" "read / A wondrous lesson in [the] silent face[s]"
("Hyperion" 3.111–12) of Mnemosyne and Moneta, respectively. Each protagonist discovers himself in the role of poet by reading the human drama
presented by his goddess; significantly, this reading process changes in the
revised version. In the first poem, there is a simple inflow of vision from
the divine text (Mnemosyne) to the human reader (Apollo) by way of "answers"; in the second, we find a more complex and reciprocal flow of questions and answers between the two (Moneta and the Poet), so that reading
becomes progressively democratic. In each case, however, reading is presented as an exercise in self-discovery. The poems can also be examined for
the various roles of poets presented: Hyperion as "man of power," or poet
of the "egotistical sublime"; Apollo as "man of genius," or the "camelion
poet"; and the Poet of "The Fall" as someone trying different roles in a
search for self. Finally, I ask students to consider these works as fragments,
incomplete texts that point in certain directions but leave the reader hanging
in a more obvious way than the earlier works did.

As a conclusion to the course, I turn to Keats's great odes. Obviously,
poems of this complexity and importance can withstand an array of approaches; but since even the reader-response perspective cannot be ade-
quately covered here, I will limit myself to a few suggestions. Two of the
odes invite response: "Nightingale" closes with two questions concerning
the validity of imagined vision, and "Grecian Urn" concludes with a cryptic
statement apparently offering, but at the same time subverting, definitive
meaning. Both works remain preoccupied with conflicts unreconciled, questions unanswered. In contrast, "Psyche" presents a sublimely vague mental
landscape as the area in which any individual's creative potential can be
fulfilled. Lastly, "Autumn" leaves maximum room for reader participation.
The poem gives us crystalized images with almost no overt message; it has

no "palpable design upon us" as it triggers our "voyage of conception." The success of "Autumn" in eliminating the obvious presence of the poet introduces questions that can be considered throughout the course: How successfully does Keats implement his own axioms regarding the writing and reading of poetry? Does he achieve the status of poet of genius, or does he slip into the role of poet of power?

Finally, on the topic of power, I cannot stress too much that an approach emphasizing the readers' (i.e., the students') responses must be grounded in the instructor's resistance to adopting the role of author(ity) of the "egotistical sublime."

THEMATIC ORIENTATIONS

Relating Keats's Myth-Oriented Poems
to Their Sources

Wolf Z. Hirst

Although I continue to use critical methods in which I was trained, I like to refresh my teaching with new perspectives. For example, J. Douglas Kneale's essay on Wordsworth and Milton, in the MLA Approaches series, shows that by concentrating on "texts and their techniques of quotation, reference, allusion, and echo," one can "extract a teaching method" from interpretations based on modern theories of intertextuality (120, 122). But it is equally valid to reconsider a method that has fallen into disuse. I here describe how a reading of several Keats poems in relation to their source myths may aid us in reassessing the poet's creative consciousness. I first discuss *Endymion* and then consider more briefly other myth-oriented poems.

My students are often struck by the brusque finale of *Endymion*, where the Indian maiden, transformed into the golden-haired goddess, abruptly disappears with her lover, who leaves his sister Peona alone "in wonderment" (4.1003). When I ask them what precisely has happened, their descriptions vary. They cheer up when I mention that critics diverge even more widely on this point than they do: some find the protagonist "is now a deity" (Harrison 554); he and Cynthia "ascend the skies together" (Matthews 142), leaving Peona behind "on earth" (Midzunoe 149); others emphasize the "subdued" tone of the close (Colvin 197), in which "the two lovers merely slip quietly away together through the woods" (Sperry 112); and "Endymion is never 'ensky'd' " (Patterson, *Daemonic* 92; cf. R. Sharp 176; Waldoff 44).

Occasionally these contrary impressions are reconciled: "there is no enskying. Or, rather, it is implied but not dramatized" (Gradman 19). I usually
let class discussion gravitate toward some such compromise. Students are
to recall Venus's vow that "'twill not be long" till Endymion has "Escap'd
from dull mortality's harsh net" (3.908, 3.907) and the prophetic dream
intimating a pledge that the hero "Would . . . win / An immortality, and
. . . espouse / Jove's daughter" (4.378–80). I then try to convince the op-
timists that these assurances have not been carried out, at least not literally,
and the pessimists, who claim the vows will never be fulfilled, that neither
have the promises been explicitly repudiated. A consensus is sometimes
reached when we return to Sidney Colvin's view that "the poem ends on
no such note of joy and triumph over the attained consummation as we might
have expected" (204). Cheated of a promised apotheosis, a number of students see the ending as a failure of Endymion's quest. At this stage I point
out something that should be obvious: as even Colvin admits, a final consummation *has* taken place. "Consummation" may be too strong a term, but
Endymion has been reunited with his goddess and in this sense has attained
his goal: perfect love, ideal beauty, a poet's immortality, and so on. In short,
the poem ends happily.

Since we always deal with some of Keats's more mature poems before
coming to *Endymion*, my students recognize that its happy ending goes
against the Keatsian pattern in which a mortal flees to an immortal dreamland
and then returns to awaken on the cold hillside of actuality. This absence
of a final ironic distancing to counterbalance the blissful bower world and
undermine dreams of immortality may be the reason reviewers and critics,
repeating the term Keats himself used in his revised preface, fault the poem
for its "mawkishness." But if the poet is so dissatisfied with his romance and
presumably with its un-Keatsian idyllic close, why does he not conclude his
story tragically, as in "Isabella," "La Belle Dame sans Merci," and "Lamia,"
or at least with an impression of transience and death, as in the last stanza
of "The Eve of St. Agnes"? After all, even though he is still, according to
his announced program, in "the realm . . . / Of Flora, and old Pan" ("Sleep
and Poetry" 101–02), Keats writes with the full consciousness of "grief contain'd / In the very deeps of pleasure" (*Endymion* 2.823–24); and the reference to "Truth the best music" (*Endymion* 4.773) proves that he has already
mastered the art of undercutting his own fictions "For truth's sake" ("Lamia"
1.395).

Before we consider the poet's decision to let *Endymion* end happily, we
should remind our students that this union between a mortal and a goddess
accords with the ancient myth and constitutes the "one bare circumstance"
to be expanded into a romance of four thousand lines (*Letters* 1: 170). In a
letter outlining the basic story to his sister, Keats describes how the moon

goddess "at last could not refrain from car[r]ying him [the 'young handsome Shepherd'] away in her arms" (*Letters* 1: 154). Still, if we find the happy ending un-Keatsian, all the more so if we feel that the poet shares our dissatisfaction, it is not enough to say that Keats follows the myth. The question to ask is why he does not deprive his hero (and his readers) of the promised final reunion—for example, by letting Endymion awaken once more from a dream—and does not leave the goddess in a distant heaven and the mortal on earth. Keats might even reverse the mythical ending by having Cynthia reject Endymion. One may object that a poet who adapts a classical myth in 1818 can deviate from his source only up to a point; and to stand the fable on its head would make nonsense of it and render it unacceptable to his audience. But such a reversal is not unknown in the literature of the period: instead of reconciling Prometheus with Jupiter-Zeus, Shelley overthrows the Olympian; Byron's Don Juan is chased by women; and Goethe's Faust goes to heaven. Nevertheless, in retelling a story, particularly a mythological one, a writer feels a certain pressure to follow its essential plot and character pattern. When we compare a literary work with its source, we must consider the author's struggle with tradition and focus on his or her characteristics, conflicts, and unique contribution to the myth, his or her originality, in a sense. Most of all, however, we must wonder what quality in the original tale led to its appropriation.

Keats's surrender to his source undoubtedly runs counter to his sense of reality. He knows that a mortal who tries to escape into a transcendental realm by embracing an immortal is doomed to disillusionment. Our former question therefore becomes more acute: Why does Keats adhere to the myth's happy end if it betrays what has been "proved upon our pulses" (*Letters* 1: 279)? And if he cannot resist the pressure of his source, why does he attempt a poem whose theme will run counter to his deepest convictions? There is one answer to these questions: the happy end of the Endymion myth serves as a license to tell a lie that satisfies his innermost cravings. He cannot literally believe that "earthly love has power to make / Men's being mortal, immortal" (1.843–44), but he *wants* to believe it. The Endymion myth—"That sweetest of all songs" he calls it in "I stood tip-toe" (182)— attracts him because it tells a lovely tale in which he would like to place his faith, though he knows it to be untrue. This gap between desire and knowledge accounts for the abrupt—perhaps strained—ending, which turns out to be less exultantly triumphant than anticipated. It also explains why scholars point to Keats's vacillation in the course of the poem (Allen 46–47; Godfrey 36; Ward 145; Evert 175; Dickstein 128; Chatterjee 260; Sperry 112; Ende 95). When Keats later confesses that the poem was "written independently *without Judgment*" (*Letters* 1: 374), he may be thinking of his misgivings about telling a falsehood in which he so desperately wants to believe.

Fidelity to his source allows Keats to eat his cake and have it too. *Endymion* both affirms and healthily questions faith. The myth appeases the transcendent longings of its hero (and, by proxy, Keats's) and yet leaves him free to broach the view that human aspiration is futile (2.142–59) and sorrow inevitable (4.146–290). Without an ultimate disillusion, the romance perfectly satisfies the poet's vague yearning for eternal love and happiness, but at the same time he recognizes that his goal is attainable only in a fairyland like Endymion's. On the one hand, "the beautiful mythology of Greece" (preface), hallowed by tradition, supplies a fiction that permits Keats to escape the harsh facts of life and indulge his secret desires; on the other, it protects him against the reproaches of his pulses and of his consecutive reasoning. Long before completing the poem, Keats sees *Endymion* as a potential tragedy of wasting youth, of fatal love and cloying pleasure, of disenchanted awakening and death; but the ancient myth directs him toward the wish-fulfillment ending of romance.

After the students arrive at this understanding, discussion may go in many directions. Is Keats at fault in rejecting the tragic outcome that he has felt upon the pulses? Or should we rather admire him for his courage in taking a project he has outgrown from the start and making of it "a test, a trial of [his] powers of Imagination" (*Letters* 1: 169) and for his negative capability in adopting an attitude toward dreams, love, and happiness that, he knows, cannot be sustained? Or is the poem's escapism irrelevant to our appreciation, because "the sense of Beauty overcomes every other consideration" (*Letters* 1: 194)? If we disparage *Endymion* for its failure to awake us from its dreamworld, are we not exposing all poetry to censure by denying it our willing suspension of disbelief? Some students may simply place a limit on their Coleridgean poetic faith and measure *Endymion* by the standard of the poet's subsequent works, condemning him for failure to counterbalance his escapist impulse with a firmer grip on reality. This approach is possible, but its far-reaching implications should be recognized. The critique encompasses, for example, the whole fairy-tale genre because it refuses to see the cathartic uses of enchantment for adults as for children (see Bettelheim). It seems strange to deny Keats the right to retell his beloved Endymion fable without reversing the traditional ending. But perhaps certain ancient myths need such a radical revision to appeal to the modern sensibility.

While virtually all Keats's important poems reflect his yearning for transcendence of mortal bounds or for union with an ideal other, no source plot apart from that of Cynthia and Endymion urges him on to a close belied by his feelings. Isabella dies broken-hearted, and "The Eve of St. Agnes" ends on a tragic or at least an ambivalent note. In "Lamia," while rewriting the myth as "sexual fantasy" (Baker 39), as his own "experience in love" (Pettet 230), or as "brutish" initiation into sex, "dehumanization of sensuality," and threat to male freedom (Van Ghent 115, 118, 122), Keats intensifies the catastrophe he finds in Burton (where the protagonist survives the disappearance of his snake-bride), though he merely has to take over the basic plot to show the futility of attempting to escape human limitations. Disastrous unions with otherworldly beings—"knights enchanted" by "a supramortal female" (Patterson, *Daemonic* 127)—also occur in some of the Renaissance legends that are partial models for "La Belle Dame sans Merci." Only in the tale of Psyche and Cupid does the poet again narrate a story that contradicts his experience of reality; this myth (Keats's favorite after Cynthia and Endymion) also ends with the enskying of a mortal. But in his "Ode to Psyche" he bypasses the problem by creating a new myth: instead of retelling the tale of a girl's loss and eventual reunion with the god of love (for which I refer students to lines 141–50 of "I stood tip-toe"), he provides a sequel beginning with a vision of the "winged" (6)—that is, already immortalized —Psyche in the arms of Cupid, and he replaces the narrative of Psyche's former earthly tribulations with the promise of worship internalized as the delightful-painful workings of the poet's imagination. Unlike *Endymion*, the ode is not vulnerable to the charge of sentimental wish fulfillment, since Psyche's triumphant anticipation of "warm Love" (67) celebrates not the poet's vicarious attainment of immortal bliss in a divine embrace but rather his confidence in the creative power of the mind and his success in recapturing visions, in translating dreams into poetry, and in overcoming the burden of the past (Bate, *Burden*) by "clearing imaginative space for himself" (Bloom, *Map* 152).

In his two versions of the Hyperion myth, Keats again fleshes out "one bare circumstance"—the overthrow of the Titans by the Olympians—and resumes the immortalization theme of *Endymion*. The titanomachy lacks the union between human being and deity depicted in the myths of Endymion and Psyche, a union symbolizing the conquest of mortal limitations and a fusion of time and eternity. Nevertheless, in his treatment of the fallen Titans, the apotheosis of Apollo, and the dreamer-narrator confronting Moneta in Saturn's temple, Keats strives to reaffirm "the victory of timelessness" and "the immortalizing power of the artist" (Hirst 96, 150). But he abandons both Hyperion poems in fragmentary form, which seems to indicate that something within him resists the vision "That first in beauty should be first in might" ("Hyperion" 2.229) and that the poet's "weak mortality" ("The Fall of Hyperion" 1.389) can bear and outlast the burden of time. It intrigues some students that Keats leaves off the second version precisely at the moment he composes "To Autumn," his supreme expression of the victory of time and natural process (see *Letters* 2: 167). Unlike the bare circumstance of the Endymion myth, the titanomachy provides no "alibi" or pretext for escaping into a sphere of eternity accessible to the artist: in "Hyperion" Keats grafts this concept on to the inherited story.

After students have learned that "Hyperion," like several other major Romantic poems, was written in revisionary strife with *Paradise Lost* (see esp. Sherwin), I try to make them aware not only of literary, cultural, and religious differences between the two poems but also of the divergent pattern of their sources. Depending on our sympathies, the overthrow of the Titans is fortunate or ill-fated, but the promise of Christian redemption can only be regarded as propitious. Milton's epic, faithful to its source, must move toward a hopeful conclusion. I usually fail to convince my audience (though I stimulate debate) that Keats could have met Milton on the latter's ground by expressing his own notions of cosmic change and individual regeneration—the defeat of time by beauty or of mortality by the artist— as the victory of Christ rather than Christ-like Apollo, or as the struggle of Christ rather than that of the agonizing dreamer-poet; Keats would then have completed his poem by yielding, as in *Endymion*, to the happy ending of a plot that has the conquest of mortality built into it. But I do get my students to concede that *Paradise Lost* and the story on which it is based are cast in a more optimistic mold than the titanomachy. Some of them even agree that the Christian story of salvation, in which Keats does not believe, might have given him an excuse—as did the Endymion myth—for wishful thinking and for resisting the sense of mortality felt on his pulses. And most members of the class begin to see that not only how a source is treated but also which source is chosen matters more than they realized.

The Envisioning of Women:
From *Endymion* to the Later Romances

Nancy Moore Goslee

In view of the verbal richness and thematic complexity of Keats's later poetry, the teacher of a course for English majors or other upper-division students must carefully weigh what to do with *Endymion*. With students often already prepared to see the Romantics as sappy escapists, the teacher who uses Keats's apprentice work to measure how far he moved beyond it may simply distort their experience of the later work. Christopher Ricks's approach through the rhetoric of the socially indiscreet does transform our sense of the poem's images and rhymes. But we still face the problems of how to relate the poem's lush surface to its thought-provoking narrative and how to relate the poem to the condensed narrative of Keats's own development. If we help students compare the relationships between the questing male figure and several types of visionary women, we can conceptualize—if not fully allegorize—the narrative of *Endymion*. We can also offer a model for interpreting Keats's later uses of romance narrative and—in other genres —romance motifs.

Endymion and its successors in Keats's experiments with romance cast the woman as other or as alien to male subjectivity—a situation so basic to Celtic myths of the elfin queen and to classical myths of the triple goddess that we tend to overlook the gender implications. Such implications have recently been explored, however, by thinkers from Simone de Beauvoir to Sherry B. Ortner to Jacques Lacan. In the first meeting of my course I introduce the narrative quest for the visionary woman as a central pattern in both Keats's and Shelley's poetry. Keats, I suggest, draws on classical and medieval versions of this pattern to develop narratives that balance "the visionary and the erotic" (Sperry 100). Are these stories about sexual experience, love, and relationship, or are they stories that use such experience to symbolize the search for transcendent imaginative vision? To clarify the pattern, I may use Blake's "Crystal Cabinet" (Parker 174; Frye, *Study* 140) and Scott's ballad version of "Thomas the Rhymer." Francis James Child's variants of both ballad and its parallel romance show how such visits to an otherworld under the hill link seduction to vision—and how the variants give the initiative sometimes to the minstrel-quester and sometimes to the elfin queen. Because "Thomas the Rhymer" relates the quest to the achievement of poetic or prophetic voice, students can discuss how such an adventure creates a poet and how such a pattern makes assumptions about gender roles. A useful effect of introducing the elfin queen or enchantress of medieval romance early in the course is that it defamiliarizes the classical myths of gods pursuing mortals and of mortals pursuing gods. For late-eighteenth-

and early-nineteenth-century knowledge of older romances, I use Arthur Johnston's *Enchanted Ground.*

Keats's interpretations of classical myth and specifically of the Endymion myth can emerge effectively from comparison of "Sleep and Poetry" with "I stood tip-toe." The first proposes a theory of transcendent inspiration mediated through sleep; the second enacts a playful conversion of natural objects into animate mythic forces. In the final example of this conversion a poet gazing at the moon transforms it into a goddess and gives her the human lover Endymion. A question for students to keep in mind as they turn to *Endymion*, then, is whether we should interpret that mysterious woman who visits the sleeping shepherd as wish fulfillment, as transcendent visitation, or as an alternative suggested by other theories of myth: etiology, euhemerism, or social projection. Before reading *Endymion*, my students will have explored the same problem in reading Shelley's *Alastor.*

At first glance *Alastor* and *Endymion* seem unlike the quest romances students may have read in Malory or other medieval writers. These Romantic poems also seem unlike the dream-visions of Chaucer or Dante. Yet because the male protagonist dreams of a beautiful, superhumanly perfect woman and then wanders in search of her, we should not be put off by the lack of a medieval setting. Keats even calls *Endymion* "A Poetic Romance," and he achieves part of the distancing characteristic of a medieval romance by using the temporally and spatially remote location of ancient Greek pastoral. Like the Elizabethans he combines Greek pastoral mythology and medieval forms of romance; like Spenser he fuses the classical mythology of an elusive virginal goddess with the medieval, romantic mythology of the elfin queen or fairy mistress. While Spenser's fairy queen represents only the benign, if mysterious, side of this medieval fusion—a side often characterized as the Lady of the Lake—his Duessa and Acrasia represent the more malign side, often characterized as Morgan le Fay.

Endymion's dream of Cynthia, then, already has a history fraught with ambiguity. Tested in his 1817 poems as a paradigm for mythmaking, the story presents problems of interpretation for its protagonist as well as for its students. Even given the complexity of Spenser's *Faerie Queene*, allegorical naming often guides the reader, if not always the knight, toward judgments. In reading Keats's poem, students should recognize that some of their resistance to the improbabilities of such stories is built into the narrative mode. Protagonists have little evidence for identifying, validating, or understanding the women they encounter except through the doubling and tripling of such figures, their exchanges of identities, and their relationships with puzzled, questing mortal men.

In book 1, the students' problem is to work between what Endymion experiences and tries to understand and what we as teachers can tell them of his myth. As in *The Faerie Queene* and other narratives of elfin queens (Paton 52), the male protagonist sleeps on a grassy bank and dreams of the woman he will then be driven to search for. Endymion also tells his sister of two subsequent moments of presence, if not of full vision, that urge him to begin his quest. Several passages in book 1, some in dramatic speech accessible to Endymion, some in narrative accessible only to readers, provide contexts for evaluating these appearances. In the earliest of these interpretive passages (1.1–33), the narrator offers the reader a working hypothesis for combining transcendent and earthly impulses, but it faces almost immediate challenge. The Latmians' hymn to Pan (1.247–306) establishes the values of a pastoral and hunting culture, immersed in the processes of earth but open to impulses from above. When Endymion explains to his sister his restless inability to participate in that world, her challenge to the validity of his dream prompts Endymion to a third interpretive passage (1.769–857), a philosophic defense that has provided the basis for Platonic and sensuous readings alike (Evert 112–22). Since the writing of this passage was for Keats an imaginative breakthough (*Letters* 1: 218), questions to ask students about these conflicting readings might run along the following lines: Like Diotima's speech in Plato's *Symposium*, this "pleasure thermometer" seems to place different kinds of love in hierarchical order. Does Endymion's discursive, if ecstatic, claim of "fellowship with essence" suggest that the visionary woman stands for something else—some ultimate idea of beauty or insight into the universe? Is this "something else" objectively real or subjectively constructed? (Ende xiv). If we interpret the woman as symbol of this something else, is she elevated or reduced? How is Endymion's placing of heterosexual love in this hierarchy different from Plato's? Is this a relationship between human and human, human and ideal, or human and goddess? With dramatic irony, we know that Endymion's dreamed-of woman is a goddess, though we can accept that knowledge less easily than Endymion might: he clearly believes in the objective existence of gods and goddesses.

In books 2 and 3, Endymion's quest roughly follows otherworld journeys both in classical epic and in medieval romance. As in many of the medieval journeys, he begins at a "shady spring" (2.53), is lured by a water nymph to a "splashing fountain's side" (2.84–85), then goes underground, and finally travels through a water passage. Moreover, the underground realm seems to possess the unreal "glamour" described in ballads or romances (Wimberly 139–61; Child nos. 4, 9, 15, 38, 39, 41). In none but mermaids' ballads does any quester actually live underwater (Slote, *Keats* 22–25); but in most underworld or otherworld journeys described in the medieval romances, the quester passes through water or blood. Boat voyages mark the transition to the enchantress's realm in the Renaissance epics of Ariosto, Tasso, and Spenser.

More important than the physical setting is the series of divine or semi-divine female figures who encounter mortal men in these underground or across-the-water unearthly places. If asked to describe the representation of women in book 2, students will probably list four figures—perhaps five, if they count the statue of Diana and Endymion's mystery woman separately. Treating Arethusa as both a stand-in for the virginal Cynthia and as a transitional figure pointing toward the ocean of book 3, we can follow Van Ghent's suggestion (ch. 2) that Endymion encounters all aspects of the ancient triple goddess: Cybele, Venus, Cynthia. By this time, the mystery woman has hinted strongly that she is constrained to secrecy because she contravenes her virginal nature and her ancient hymns—in other words, that she is the moon goddess and huntress to whom Endymion has been praying for relief. Is Endymion given a survey of women whose roles and powers seem defined by fertility? Does that perspective increase his passivity, strengthen their identity as impersonal biological functions? If so, Cynthia's rebellion may be a step toward a more personal, individuating relationship.

As students are quick to point out, Alpheus's more active pursuit of Arethusa distinguishes their relationship from that of Venus and Adonis and of Endymion and Cynthia—and would distinguish it from any male's relationship with Cybele, if Keats had described one in detail. The parallel of Endymion and Adonis, a figure like "might half slumb'ring on its own right arm" ("Sleep and Poetry" 237), may seem to suggest that beautiful young men are aesthetic objects or sexual fetishes to these goddesses. Barbara A. Schapiro's discussions of narcissism in *The Romantic Mother* can point to a preliminary comparison of Endymion's two major encounters with his visionary goddess—in his dream (1.578–678) and waking from his dream (2.707–853)—to the visionary's encounter with his dream visitant in *Alastor*.

Book 3 works toward answers both to the Adonis-like passivity and to the obsessive, solipsistic focus of the *Alastor* visionary by casting Endymion as a humanitarian. How satisfying is this solution, though? Students might discuss how they would dramatize such a development. In Keats's version, Endymion does show sympathy to Glaucus after an initial revulsion, but his subsequent acts, such as sprinkling pieces of the shredded prophetic scroll over the drowned lovers, seem purely formulaic. Like Perceval's second, more sympathetic response to the fisher king's plight in the Grail castle, this moment of sympathy leads almost arbitrarily to new life and a promise of restored fertility for all.

Yet Endymion is excluded. Keats had, as critics repeatedly note, more lines to write (Bate, *John Keats* 169). If we see Glaucus's involvement with

Scylla and Circe as an analysis of the conflicts implicit in book 2, we can also see it as pointing toward Endymion's conflict in book 4. Though the names Scylla and Circe come from that oceanic protoromance *The Odyssey*, Keats probably borrows more directly from Ovid (*Metamorphoses* 14; see also Bush, *Renaissance Tradition* 83–85). Drawing on that narrative, he uses its two opposing stereotypes for women, especially for women as portrayed in romances—the pursued damsel and the entrapping enchantress. It is as if the dominating aspect of Venus joins the witchlike aspect of Cybele and opposes the traditional elusive virgin. In book 3, Glaucus's aggressive pursuit of Scylla follows almost immediately his aggressive, but more speculative, leap into the ocean, as though further manifesting or anthropomorphizing those "distemper'd longings" (3.375). As in Ovid, Glaucus appears from the beginning to know that Circe is an enchantress and to seek her out for that reason. Yet in *Endymion*, either he does not know the full extent of her magic or he does not recognize Circe in the beautiful stranger who seduces him (Bush, *Romantic Tradition* 91), until he stumbles into the scene with her enthralled animals. Thus he becomes more like those protagonists in the medieval romances and the Renaissance romantic epics who naively wander into an enchantress's bower and are trapped there. In Ovid, Glaucus rudely rejects the advances of Circe, and she, in revenge, changes Scylla into a hideous misogynist version of her own aggressive sexuality—a beauty from the waist up, but belted around with barking dogs. Keats's Glaucus submits to Circe; and when he later resists, her punishment is to make him less animal than before by making him endlessly old. Keats turns the story toward a patient endurance—completed after a millennium—that makes possible Glaucus's eventual reconciliation with a resurrected Scylla. Both his submission to Circe and his patient rehabilitation point toward Endymion's experiences in book 4 (Parker 178).

The opposition between Cynthia and the Indian maid in book 4 recalls the original tension between transcendence and an arcadian, Pan-like process in book 1. Yet Endymion's education in sympathy and in action is further tested by a new version of Glaucus's narrative. Because Cynthia is elusive, she resembles Scylla; because the Indian maid is a follower of pleasure and of Dionysus and seems very available, she resembles Circe and her intemperate physicality. Leading Endymion to become unfaithful to his ideal love, she makes him fall from his heavenly aspirations. Morris Dickstein reads this as a necessary, fortunate fall into a world of experience and tragedy; it makes possible the revelation of Cynthia as a higher understanding (106) and saves the logic of the myth. Yet students who have read *Alastor* should compare Endymion's rejection of the apparently unattainable goddess with the opposite choice made by Shelley's visionary. Scarcely noticing a devoted

Arab maid, Shelley's quester continues the futile pursuit of his dream woman. In this context, Endymion's rejection of dream for earthbound reality is not a fall but a moral choice to affirm humanity.

With Cynthia's apotheosis, however, the Indian maid becomes the false image. Is Endymion now rewarded for making the right choice, by being given the wrong reward? Is he rewarded for making the wrong choice, by being given the right prize? Does his moral commitment to humanity and to earth, rejecting the vague transcendence of dream-vision, receive confirmation through the conventional and transcendentalized aesthetic object of the blond goddess? A comparison with the romance of the loathly lady, the most familiar example of which is Chaucer's Wife of Bath's Tale, will surely lead to further discussion—though not likely to neat answers. All these problems are to some extent anticipated in the oxymoron of pleasure and sorrow first voiced by the Indian maid, though her statements do not incorporate the issue of humanitarian commitment that Endymion brings to the relationship. Nor does the poem's sudden conclusion do so. It seems to make Endymion and Cynthia local deities who, though they live in the woods and not in heaven, barely touch human lives.

In this way Endymion comes even more to resemble the questers who venture into an elfin queen's realm, share its visionary "glamour," and cannot ever fully return to human encounters. Like Thomas the Rhymer, they may gain prophetic power, but they gain it only through alienation. According to this reading, Cynthia is the Circe figure, having absorbed the symbolism of alienating enchantment associated with the Indian maid. Most paradoxically, Cynthia seems to achieve her power by being recognized as a dream—that is, Endymion recognizes his own myth as an imaginative fiction, dismisses it, and then finds that it has new power. She thus looks ahead to La Belle Dame, to Lamia, and—in complex ways—to Madeline in "The Eve of St. Agnes." A brief look at these three poems suggests possibilities for further discussion of these patterns (see Rajan 97–101).

In "La Belle Dame," the elusive damsel and the Circean enchantress are ambiguously fused in the role of an archetypal elfin queen. Comparing the poem with "Thomas the Rhymer" or with Thomas Chester's *Launfal*, another medieval romance, shows how the protagonist's relationship with the fairy mistress is at odds with the social world he has wandered away from. Is the knight's simultaneous waking from his dream of society's judgment and from the grotto similar to Endymion's dismissal of Cynthia as a torturing, irrelevant vision? Instead of being rewarded for his awakening, the knight is haunted by the figure he seemed to reject, but, in contrast to Cynthia's speech, no voice or image gives her viewpoint (Kelley 336, 342; Swann 87, 90). Asking students to judge the intentions and the subjectivity of the mysterious woman encourages them to look ahead to the "Grecian Urn," "Melancholy," and the two Hyperion poems, where the narrators or gods grasp for a woman's alienated consciousness. Finally, if the knight's dream leads to an attempt to categorize the lady, to make her either an elusive Diana or an enthralling Morgan or Circe, in what category should we place the lingering knight? His liminal state seems to confirm both the lady's and the poem's resistance to analysis, a resistance that retains magical power.

Like *Endymion*, "The Eve of St. Agnes" involves a sleeper who wakes to find a dream real and lit in a silvery, if chilling, moonlight. The name of the dreamer is an excellent starting point for a discussion that pursues the categories of women that Keats has tested and complicated in *Endymion*: the Magdalene whose name is also that of the virginal Mary. Jack Stillinger's critique of Earl R. Wasserman's idealistic reading might be reinterpreted not just to replace a neo-Platonist reading with a Machiavellian one but to recognize that both readings "hoodwink" the consciousness of the woman's subjectivity—or at least hoodwink readers into being unable to see it (Stillinger, *Hoodwinking* 67–93; Wasserman 97–137). Both Porphyro and Madeline fantasize about the other as object, but Madeline in her dreaming and waking more closely resembles Endymion and the knight in "La Belle Dame." Her sad acceptance of the actual, pallid Porphyro brings about an apotheosis the reverse of Cynthia's—he becomes the warmer, more vital lover of her dreams. Do the categories posed by Cynthia and the Indian maid, Scylla and Circe, have, then, no relevance to Madeline, given this reversal? Or does her capacity to dream the witchlike enchantment or shape changing grant her a goddess's power and thus make Porphyro, for all his aggressiveness, again the passive Endymion? Their vanishing into the storm leaves them, too, in a liminal state, as if even their mutual definitions can evade analysis.

Both in couplets and in analytical method of characterization, "Lamia" returns to *Endymion*. Through its urbane tone, it seems to develop an urban version of the elfin-queen motif; the otherworld fairy hall exists in the interstices of a Corinthian neighborhood. Lamia's Circean powers of metamorphosis would appear to tilt the balance so perfectly created in "La Belle Dame" toward a sensual malevolence, particularly since Lycius has abandoned his pursuit of philosophical truth to live in her palace. She thus seems a powerful goddess-figure encouraging, like Cynthia and Venus, the passivity of her lover and yet more resistant than they to idealization. How does Lycius's new skepticism of her reality at the wedding feast compare with the skepticism of Endymion in book 4, of the knight in the grotto, or of Madeline in her bed? Lycius's invitation to society, whether egotistic or altruistic, breaks the taboo against making such enchantment public; yet it is the challenge of the philosopher Apollonius that breaks that synthesis so precariously worked out in *Endymion* and so mysteriously, powerfully evaded in the other two poems: the synthesis of visionary love as a form of knowledge. Lamia, once a playful Circe, becomes a snakelike victim of this extreme categorization.

Keats and the Music of Mortality

Ronald A. Sharp

A few years ago E. L. Doctorow returned to Kenyon College for a memorial celebration of his friend and classmate James Wright. As he affectionately recalled their student days together, Doctorow told a wonderful story about himself and Wright, both of whom considered themselves serious writers as undergraduates. They were walking through the campus, approaching a group of students whom they regarded as "pseudopoets," phony pretenders to the literary who were really just sentimental half-wits. It was autumn and the ground was covered with leaves. As the pseudopoets approached, Doctorow leaped dramatically into a pile of leaves, threw a handful up in the air, and, as they began to fall around him, sang out in his best mock-poetic tone, "The leaves, the leaves are falling"—making fun of the kind of poetry that these phonies would write.

Doctorow and Wright maintained their friendship; and thirty years later, when Wright lay on his deathbed in a New York hospital, he had a visit from his old schoolmate. Wright, now in the last stages of cancer of the mouth, was unable to speak. After they embraced, Wright scrawled a few words on a piece of paper and handed it to Doctorow. It said: "The leaves are falling." Wright died a few days later.

I begin my teaching of Keats by telling the students this story (which, in a different form, Doctorow repeats in his *Lives of the Poets*) and then reading to them from a letter that Keats wrote to James Rice a week after his first hemorrhage and a year before his death:

> How astonishingly (here I must premise that illness as far as I can judge in so short a time has relieved my Mind of a load of deceptive thoughts and images and makes me perceive things in a truer light)— How astonishingly does the chance of leaving the world impress a sense of its natural beauties on us. Like poor Falstaff, though I do not babble, I think of green fields. I muse with the greatest affection on every flower I have known from my infancy—their shapes and coulours as are new to me as if I had just created them with a superhuman fancy. . . . The simple flowers of our sp[r]ing are what I want to see again.
>
> (*Letters* 2: 260)

Like many people facing death, Keats had a renewed sense of the wonder of the world—a feeling heightened by the prospect of an ending. This idea, at first so distant to twenty-year-olds, engages students with extraordinary intensity and takes them quickly into what I take to be the heart of Keats's tragic vision.

All students have seen reports of people in crisis who come to a new understanding of what matters to them—POWs who only want another chance to spend time with their children, highjack victims who in a flash see that their materialistic lives have been empty, the father or neighbor or aunt who, in the midst of a terminal illness, feels a love for family and friends that flows more deeply and fully than it ever did before. What I want my students to see is that a similar perspective characterized Keats's view of the world, most poignantly toward the end of his career but also in fact virtually from the beginning, long before he was actually dying. At the foundation of Keats's work is the profound paradox that a sense of mortality increases one's sense of beauty, that life accrues value precisely to the extent that one intensely experiences its fragility and transience. One good way to clarify this view for students is to focus at the outset on mortality itself, for, as Wallace Stevens says in his most Keatsian poem, "Death is the mother of beauty" ("Sunday Morning" 63, 88).

Keats's concern with death and loss comes so directly from his own experience and his story is so gripping that we should share it with our students. Undergraduates needn't be required to read a biography, but they should know about the early death of Keats's father, about the deaths of his grandparents, and especially about how Keats nursed his mother and his brother Tom during their fatal illnesses. We should also tell them about Keats's awakening Charles Brown just after dawn to tell him that Tom had died; about the moment not long afterward when Keats first spat blood and told Brown it was his "death-warrant"; about Keats's asking Joseph Severn to visit the cemetery where he would soon be buried and then listening to Severn's description of the goats and sheep there and the early wildflowers in the grass; and about the evening a few days later when Keats gasped to his friend, "Severn—I—lift me up—I am dying—I shall die easy—don't be frightened—be firm, and thank God it has come!" (Rollins 2: 94).

It is useful to begin with such stories because death is scarcely a burning issue for most young men and women, and these anecdotes provide an immediacy that leads quickly to the themes of transience and beauty. Though it is important to return, in the study of Keats, to the question of his general view of death—particularly in the late letters and in poems like "When I Have Fears," "Bright Star," "This Mortal Body," "This Living Hand," the odes, and both versions of "Hyperion"—these initial reflections are not designed to address that issue. Nor, I should add, is this brief essay an attempt to do so.

What I would like to do, however, is to look at a few widely taught works of Keats and suggest ways in which our teaching of them can be illuminated by an introductory emphasis on death. Ironically, my central example, "To Autumn," does not directly discuss human death. But death is not mentioned in "To Autumn" not because Keats is anxious about it but because he has come so fully to grips with it that it has come to have the status of the obvious and therefore needs no discussion. In this poem the speaker's awareness and acceptance of death occur at such a fully integrated level of consciousness that the outer world is rinsed of death's stain yet everywhere bears death's signature.

The natural cycles of the year and the day are moving toward winter and night, poised in the bittersweetness of autumn twilight. Against this transient background, numerous smaller cycles are playing themselves out. Nuts, fruits, and flowers are all ripe or overripe, and this "ripeness to the core" signifies the fullness of life and—what becomes virtually synonymous with that fullness—the inevitability of death. We need to show our students that underlying these bountiful images of completion is Keats's conviction that it is precisely because death is always implicated in life that life takes on its special poignance and beauty. This beauty inheres in our experience of autumn and shapes our response to its thousand details of imminent closure: the swollen gourds, the "plump . . . hazel shells," the "full-grown lambs," the "gathering swallows," the apples about to fall off the tree or to be pressed into cider. There is nothing alarming about those prospects. The "cottage-trees" bent with apples offer an image of utter abundance, of a world teeming with life (the trees are even "moss'd") and "mellow fruitfulness." Even when the apples go to the "cyder-press," the sense of an ending is inextricably tied up with a sense of their juicy life, as "with patient look, / Thou watchest the last oozings hours by hours." Keats subtly detaches autumn from any threatening association with the traditional figure of death, who indifferently mows us down with a scythe. Although he provides his figure of autumn with that same tool, he undermines any comparison with death by making autumn a gentle creature "Drows'd with the fume of poppies," whose hair is "soft-lifted by the winnowing wind" and whose scythe "Spares the next swath." The field will indeed be mowed down; death will eventually come, even to that next swath "and all its twined flowers," which the "hook" has spared only temporarily. But by embracing—not just accepting but actually embracing—mortality, Keats discovers again the paradox that death is the mother of beauty.

It is important that we spend time with our students on this distinction, and one good place to begin is with Elizabeth Kübler-Ross's celebrated work on the stages that people who are dying typically pass through. After initial periods of denial and isolation, anger, bargaining, and depression, many people reach a stage of acceptance: "It is not a resigned 'giving up,' a sense of 'what's the use' " (*Death* 99) but rather a state of "equanimity and peace" and of dignity (*Questions* 34). And yet, she says, "acceptance . . . is almost void of feelings" (*Death* 100).

The voice of "To Autumn" is clearly not one of mere resignation to death, and it is indeed characterized by peace and dignity. But so far is it from being devoid of feeling that we might well say that the genius and originality of the poem lie precisely in its rendering and orchestration of complex and profound feelings in the face of death—feelings that include peace and equanimity, to be sure, but that embrace both life and death with a heart-breaking intensity and vividness. Keats does indeed accept death, but his acceptance involves beauty because it is active rather than passive, because, like Apollo in "Hyperion," he does not merely register or admit "Knowledge enormous" but lets the experience of mortality "Pour into the wide hollows of [his] brain" (3.113, 117).

The day in "To Autumn" may be dying, but its death is figured forth as a blossoming: "barred clouds *bloom* the soft-dying day, / And touch the stubble-plains with rosy hue" (emphasis added). Keats has no fantasy here of rebirth. If autumn is beautiful, it is not because winter will be followed by spring. "Where are the songs of spring?" he asks. "Ay, where are they? / Think not of them, thou hast thy music too." Autumn's most beautiful music can be heard only when we shed our fantasies of rebirth and accept the reality of death. When we do that, the ending of a day can be seen as a sort of fruition, a coming into itself, a full flowering. The fields may then be "stubble-plains," but, seen in this light, they will take on a "rosy hue."

Examining these and other images in "To Autumn" helps students see the connection between the courageous serenity of the poem's voice and the larger conception of death and its relation to beauty. I follow a similar procedure in teaching "Ode on Melancholy," another poem that takes up this paradoxical relationship. If "To Autumn" presents a view of how the world feels to someone who has fully accepted mortality, the "Melancholy" ode backs up a step and addresses the question of how one might arrive at such a view. Unlike "To Autumn," the most unexpository and highly imagistic of the odes, "Melancholy" adopts the argumentative mode, taking as its point of departure the implied question, why one should not commit suicide. The poem's answer is directly related to the paradoxes sketched above.

The first step in getting students to see this issue is to make clear just how high the stakes are in the opening lines. Though the question of where one can find melancholy becomes crucial in the poem, at the beginning the urgent issue is how to respond to it. The point is not simply that wolfsbane and nightshade distract you from true melancholy; they kill you. These are deadly poisons. When Keats says,

> No, no, go not to Lethe, neither twist
>   Wolf's-bane, tight-rooted, for its poisonous wine;
> Nor suffer thy pale forehead to be kiss'd
>   By nightshade, ruby grape of Proserpine . . . ,

he means that when "the wakeful anguish of the soul" comes on us, when "the melancholy fit" falls on us, we should not kill ourselves. Instead, we should turn to human and natural beauties—"a morning rose," "the rainbow of the salt sand-wave," "the wealth of globed peonies," the "peerless eyes" of "thy mistress"—and experience them with intensity ("feed deep, deep").

But if beauty can console us in our melancholy, it can never do so permanently, for by definition beauty fades: the lovely peonies will soon be "droop-headed" again, so that the "morning" in "morning rose" emerges as a pun on "mourning," and even the "rainbow of the salt sand-wave" reveals its association with the salty tears of the "weeping cloud" of melancholy. But that same "weeping cloud" "fosters" the flowers in the first place. Though it is sad that beauty must die, that "Joy['s] . . . hand is ever at his lips / Bidding adieu," this transience gives beauty its meaning. We need to emphasize that this is not simply an elaborate aesthetic paradox but a hard-won human insight. Far from being a ridiculously idealistic "romantic" speculation, as some students might think, it is the existential foundation for Keats's rejection of suicide.

Here we might remind our students how tough-minded Keats was about death. In "Ode to a Nightingale," for example, he feels pain and loss so intensely that he admits, "I have been half in love with easeful Death" and "Now more than ever seems it rich to die" (52, 55); and in "Why did I laugh tonight?" he says, "death is life's high meed." Whatever affirmations Keats discovers can never insulate him fully against the sorrow of loss. In this respect death is only the most extreme form of the perennial problem of loss and human pain. From the beginning of his career the inevitability of suffering runs relentlessly through Keats's poems and letters. "Such is this World," he tells Bailey as early as 1817, "and we live . . . in a continual struggle against the suffocation of accidents" (*Letters* 1: 179). "Pleasure is oft a visitant," says Endymion, "but pain / Clings cruelly to us" (1.906–07). Keats understands that a poet who has not come to grips with these dark realities has no right to become a spiritual physician. "None can usurp this height," says Moneta in "The Fall of Hyperion," "But those to whom the miseries of the world / Are misery, and will not let them rest" (1.147–49).

It is in the "vale of Soul-making" letter that Keats develops this argument most fully, and I would strongly urge that it be assigned to students in conjunction with "To Autumn" and "Ode on Melancholy." For in that letter Keats is explicit: "Do you not see how *necessary* a World of Pains and troubles is to school an Intelligence and make it a soul?" (*Letters* 2: 102; emphasis added). Suffering is not simply an evil that one has to bear but the prerequisite for developing a soul.

Returning to the ode, we find that, in a similar manner, melancholy is both inescapable and necessary for the highest—or deepest—sense of beauty:

Ay, in the very temple of Delight
  Veil'd Melancholy has her sovran shrine,
    Though seen of none save him whose strenuous tongue
  Can burst Joy's grape against his palate fine. . . .

The syntactic ambiguity in those first two lines is crucial. In one sense, it is distressing that even in the temple of *delight* one finds melancholy: beauty and joy are indeed ephemeral. But in another sense, it is critical that melancholy's shrine is in the temple not of despair but of delight, for it is the fact of transience that makes beauty meaningful.

Still, the only people who can see that beauty are those who burst joy's grape, that is, those who live with the kind of intensity that embraces rather than evades the painful facts of death, loss, and melancholy. They understand what Keats means in "Hyperion" when he speaks of "Sorrow more beautiful than Beauty's self" (1.36)—more beautiful because Keats discovers in the depths of suffering the most persuasive ground for affirming life. Rather than seeking oblivion when faced with melancholy, Keats suggests that if we face it head on, hug it to ourselves, we will find within it what we need to go on.

Though the notion that death should be openly discussed is becoming a cliché of popular culture, for most of our students—indeed, most Americans of any age—death remains largely something to ignore. In Keats's view, however, embracing death—not just refusing to evade it but actually embracing it as part of a world in which everything passes—somehow makes everything matter more, somehow makes everything seem more valuable. To embrace the sense of an ending throws everything into relief, makes us see with a dewy freshness even, as Keats remarked, "the simple flowers of . . . sp[r]ing." The reason those flowers are so beautiful is, if I may quote James Wright out of context, that we know it will not be long until "the leaves are falling." If we can get our students to understand that connection, we will have gone a long way toward helping them understand those "happy, happy boughs" that "cannot shed / [their] leaves" ("Grecian Urn")—and much else at the heart of Keats's tragic vision.

Romance to Ode: Love's Dream and the Conflicted Imagination

Jean Hall

In my Romantic poetry course the odes are generally the focus and culmination of our Keats studies. These frequently interpreted poems can take on freshness if they are approached through "The Eve of St. Agnes" and "Lamia"; for the tendency to see the odes simply as creations of an isolate imagination is corrected by an awareness of Keats's romances, which reflect on the social implications of the imagination as it is expressed in the dream of love.

I begin with that dream's beauty as figured in "The Eve of St. Agnes," encouraging the students to see Madeline and Porphyro as poets engaged in creating their love's world. I then turn the discussion to their rival fantasies. First I ask students to reflect on Madeline's assumptions. We trace her preparations for St. Agnes' Eve, which rely on timeworn customs requiring maidens to look neither "behind, nor sideways," to petition "heaven with upward eyes" (53, 54), to make "No uttered syllable" (203), and to go to bed supperless and devout. As the rigidity of these procedures begins to emerge, it becomes obvious that such ritualism hampers individual perception. Madeline conforms to a rule-bound regime that excludes her own seeing and saying. Asked how Porphyro's performance compares with Madeline's, students notice that he breaks all the rules to achieve his ends. Not only does he invade his enemy's castle, he persuades Angela, the nursemaid, to let him hide in Madeline's chamber and observe her preparations for bed. In the course of the evening he sees a great deal, and when Madeline falls asleep, he moves from perception to action, setting out his table of sweetmeats, singing his ballad, and finally taking Madeline herself.

When students have comprehended the immense differences between Madeline's ritualism and Porphyro's activism, I ask them to make moral evaluations of these behaviors. Jack Stillinger's influential essay "The Hoodwinking of Madeline" shows students how Porphyro's activism is a form of manipulation and an invasion of privacy—for he slips into Madeline's dream and exploits her assumptions about St. Agnes' Eve. The sexual consummation that Madeline believes she is dreaming is actually carried out, but Porphyro could not have fulfilled this love if Madeline had realized it was taking place in reality. Are we to condemn Porphyro's behavior or not?

As students grapple with this difficulty, they begin to see that if invasion of privacy is a problem posited by the poem, a hypothetical alternative—Porphyro's failure to take any action at all—might have created an equally distressing dilemma. Had that happened, the lovers would have remained confined in their separate dreams, their love's world never becoming shared and actual. And, in fact, the isolation and purity of dreams is a value promoted by Madeline's ritualistic procedures, which would have preserved her virginity at the expense of her fulfillment. Students come to recognize that Madeline's imaginative and moral purity is being purchased at the price of her divorce from reality—that her dream of love can exist only in isolation. In contrast, Porphyro's dream, though impure, based as it is on manipulation, is still a dream of a real relationship. By artfully slipping into Madeline's dream, Porphyro can take her into his own.

The poem's conclusion enacts a temporary harmony, as Madeline and Porphyro declare their mutual love and escape from her family's castle to pursue a new life together. But as students ponder this outcome, they grasp the delicate and provisional character of Keats's happy ending: what will happen to the lovers in the stormy world outside the enchanted precincts of Madeline's bedchamber? No longer in the privileged environment of their dreams, Madeline and Porphyro are moving into a world of contingencies; and if the world's ways do not defeat them, the lovers themselves may destroy their happiness. Students realize that the poem presents a dilemma: if Madeline's dreamworld is deceptive insofar as it avoids actualizing love, Porphyro's imagination actualizes love through a deception both immoral and dangerous.

It is possible to read "Lamia" as a continuing investigation of the problems raised by "The Eve of St. Agnes." Students first discover that in "Lamia" the roles of man and woman are more or less reversed: it is the woman, Lamia, who imaginatively actualizes a world of love and manipulates the man, Lycius, into inhabiting it. But in the poem's second part he breaks free of her spell. I ask students why this happens: doesn't Lycius still love Lamia, and hasn't he enjoyed living in her magic palace? Students become aware of a new element: Lycius's need for activity, for doing something more than merely enjoying Lamia's enchantments. As passive recipient of her love, he has become curiously isolated and feels the need to break free into the world outside their mutual dream. If the dream of love is shared in "Lamia," the starring role is not—for the dream is staged by one party, who becomes the creative artist, and beheld by the second party, who becomes her audience. Within the world of love, conflict inevitably arises, as the parties compete for the dominant role—and I point out that this might have happened in "The Eve of St. Agnes" if Keats had extended the poem to include Madeline and Porphyro's life together.

The remainder of "Lamia" shows Lycius's attempt to fulfill the role of creator, and I ask students to compare his performance with Lamia's. They realize that if Keats has portrayed her ambiguously as a beautiful snakewoman, he has done worse to Lycius—for there is no ambiguity, no subtlety in his raw and pathetic need to dominate. Not only will he control Lamia, Lycius also will triumph over everyone else in Corinth by flaunting Lamia as his prize in a huge public wedding. By publicizing his dream, Lycius opens the way for Apollonius to behold the lovers and dispel their world as an illusion. The final catastrophe of "Lamia," reflecting the limitations of both possibilities depicted in "St. Agnes," shows that, if love's dream cannot bear public scrutiny, neither can a private and isolated dreamworld long satisfy the dreamer's need for activity and actualization.

Tracking Keats's explorations of love's dream through the romance line of his poetry creates an interesting context for teaching the odes. The disasters of "Lamia" make it clear that the imagination is imperiled in a public world and at the same time is itself dangerous—for competing imaginative claims of different people impose on one another. But "Lamia," written a few months after the odes, throws interesting retrospective light on Keats's creative strategy in his most famous group of poems. All the odes are reflexive—each involves a speaker who turns inward, making himself into a world where the imagination's desires may be enacted. This kind of privacy is critically different from the private worlds of love in "The Eve of St. Agnes" and "Lamia," which are inhabited by two people and therefore involve potential conflicts of interest.

In "Ode to Psyche" the speaker laments the loss of a world of belief, in which the gods were seen by human beings and were worshipped in public ceremonies. The speaker himself catches a glimpse of Cupid and Psyche embracing and wants to protect the goddess by making a world fit for her habitation "In some untrodden region of my mind" (51), where he can become "Thy voice, thy lute, thy pipe, thy incense sweet . . . Thy shrine, thy grove, thy oracle" (46–48). Like Lamia, this speaker takes his beloved into a self-created world where he plays all the attendant parts necessary for her worship. Religion is converted into imagination, as the public and exterior world is replaced by the speaker's private and interior creation. This ode clearly is a meditation on the imagination, and that is why we can see the speaker's interiorization of Psyche as reverent. Keats's goddess is less a character than a symbol of the problems of belief and desire—but if she had emerged as a person, the speaker's protectiveness would have begun to look like a sort of benevolent entrapment not unlike Porphyro's seduction of Madeline or Lamia's enchantment of Lycius. Because Psyche is not a separate personality but rather an aspect of the speaker's mind, we remain untroubled by the way she is treated in this poem.

"Ode to a Nightingale" and "Ode on a Grecian Urn" also deploy elements of the self. Even more obviously than "Psyche," their objects of meditation—the nightingale and the urn—are not persons in their own right. The bird is nonhuman, an eternal song without words, and the urn's pictures render the ardent and reverent surfaces of human life without its interior. Both birdsong and urn are sheer display and that is why the odes' speakers

are free to enter them and supply them with their own inn
stratagems of Porphyro and Lamia, which could be regarded a
Madeline's and Lycius's privacy, in these odes are transformed into ⸻
acts of bestowal. Through their imaginative participation the speakers give
the objects of their meditation a living fullness that would otherwise be
lacking. The closest parallel to this effect in Keats's romances is Porphyro's
actualization of Madeline's dream—but the odes avoid the moral ambiguities
involved in Porphyro's action.

As the relation of the odes to "The Eve of St. Agnes" and "Lamia" begins
to be clear, students may raise objections to Keats's procedure: Isn't the
conversion of the world into the self, the exclusion of all persons but the
lyric "I" from poetry, a radical defensiveness? If the purification of one's
motives depends on eliminating every other person from one's world, is
purity really worth the price? Aren't the speakers of these odes repeating
Madeline's error by dwelling in dreams of the isolate imagination? These
questions should be raised not to be easily dismissed but to facilitate an
understanding of what the odes achieve and what they sidestep. Keats's
Great Odes are not social poetry as are many other major works of English
Romanticism, such as *The Prelude, Don Juan,* and *Prometheus Unbound.*
But if they are expressions of the isolate imagination that purify the self by
freeing it from social entanglements, nevertheless they do not falsify self-
representation by conveying a specious impression of harmony. The potential
destruction that can result from imposing one's imaginations on others is
converted in the odes into a reflexive theme—for here we see how the
imagination must undercut itself, twinning destruction with its creations.
What one person does to another in "The Eve of St. Agnes" or "Lamia,"
the contending parts of the self do to each other in the odes. David Perkins
has discussed the "symbolic debate" of the odes (*English Romantic Writers*),
and I would suggest that this is the isolate imagination's debate with itself
—a feature of the odes that parallels the conflict of interest between Madeline's and Porphyro's or Lamia's and Lycius's imaginations in the romances.

The well-known reversal-and-return pattern of most of the odes is a consequence of this symbolic debate. Particularly in the "Nightingale" and the
"Urn" odes, the speaker begins in isolation, moves into an imaginative one-
ness with the object of his meditation, and finally finds it necessary to return
to his sole self. The arc of his meditation becomes an interior drama in which
the competing claims of the imagination assert themselves and are under-
mined. For example, in "Nightingale" he desires to be one with the bird so
ardently that he would "cease upon the midnight with no pain, / While thou
art pouring forth thy soul abroad / In such an ecstasy!" (56–58). But if this
ecstatic moment satisfies his need to identify absolutely with the bird, he
rapidly realizes that it also deprives him of his personal existence. The

nightingale would sing on, but he would "have ears in vain—/ To thy high requiem become a sod" (59–60). The speaker's conflicting desires—for imaginative transcendence and for self-awareness—cannot be accommodated harmoniously but must interact with and reverse each other. The prolonged imaginative domination that Lamia exerts over Lycius is replaced by the swift and agile meditation of the odes, as the speaker allows his impulses freedom and his conflicting desires rapidly undercut each other.

Although this process has its destructive aspects, students need to appreciate Keats's important concept: the free play of imagination as a route to the growth of the soul. The odes may be the expression of the isolate imagination, but that imagination is crucially unlike Madeline's because it does not decree a static dreamworld divorced from actualization. Reflexivity in the odes allows for an imaginative conflict of interests that enlarges and complicates the soul's awareness and feeling and redefines actualization as the meditations of a resonant spirit. In the end the speaker of the odes returns to his sole self, as Madeline and Porphyro must leave their enchanted bedchamber and Lamia and Lycius must forfeit their dream. Students begin to realize that Keats's notion of growth intertwines imaginative pleasure and sorrow, and they should be left free to evaluate this marvelous tonal complexity for themselves.

Reading and Ravishing:
The "Ode on a Grecian Urn"

Peter J. Manning

Exploring the commonplace that we read Keats's "Ode on a Grecian Urn" as its speaker reads the urn before him makes manifest to students the play of investments and identifications, the readjustments of sympathy and distance, that they perform unself-consciously when they interpret poems—or objects, or others. By presenting reading as an act charged with desire, the poem reveals the tensions between projecting the self and seeking the other that are intrinsic to reading. In the first stanza the speaker's imagination kindles the static scene on the urn into a vision of mad pursuit and wild ecstasy: he projects his own erotic energy onto the urn, which mirrors it back to him. Even as the first stanza offers terms that represent as harmonious the transaction between object and beholder (or poem and reader)—as, for example, the adoption of a child or the consummation of a marriage—it unsettles them: the urn is a "foster-child," separated from its begetter, and the as-yet unravished bride is perhaps another maiden loath, struggling to escape her fate in the desire of the reader. The poem shows that the (male) subject's narcissistic projection constitutes a ravishing of the (female) object he represents.

Even for first-time readers the alternation in stanzas 1 and 2 between undertones of violence and affirmations of composure raises questions, which I may meet in class with a psychoanalytic interpretation that sees the relation as one of form and content and the function as defensive: as the formal beauty of the urn encompasses the passions acted out on its surface, so the intricate patterning of Keats's verse contains, and thus makes possible the uttering of, desires and fears. At the level of the encounter between beholder and object, reader and text, the stillness and the ravishing are more tightly interwoven, because it is the self-enclosure of the urn that provokes the fantasy of ravishment. The urn is represented as expressive but not communicative: the curious locution by which its "legend"—literally, that which is read, the inscription typically found on urns—appears merely as a phantom haunting about its shape underscores the (pretended) absence of connection between urn and beholder. The men or gods pursuing the nymphs, the youth who cannot leave his song, and the lover approaching his love are wholly absorbed, oblivious of anyone watching them. Students recognize the frequency of this spectatorial situation in Keats's poetry: the repeated sequences of vision, union, and swoon in *Endymion*, Porphyro entranced by the disrobing Madeline, the knight who gazed at La Belle Dame and "nothing else saw all day long," the speaker who encounters Cupid and Psyche embracing, and the dreamer transfixed by the face of Moneta ("visionless entire . . . Of all external things") in "The Fall of Hyperion" (1.267–68). As in these instances, the fascination of the urn arises directly from that indifference to the audience which its silence betokens. The urn's withdrawal at once generates its power to transfix the beholder and prevents the engagement with the other through which the self might know itself. Yet because the urn's otherness of kind is absolute, to fill that absence by projection, abolishing the distance on which desire depends, is to empty the self into a narcissistic fantasy.

Ravishing the urn and being ravished by her are two sides of the same coin, or perhaps the two projections of the urn, before and behind the frieze on its surface: the frieze denies the presence of the beholder, who in turn recuperates absence as an endless depth behind it, the virtual image of an inexhaustible richness in the urn and the poem of which it is the emblem. But it is only a virtual image, an idealizing purchased at the cost of the separate existence of the beholder. In the first two stanzas his rapt concentration on a world that ignores him threatens him with a stonelike immobility: in valuing the static silence of the urn over the narrative movement of rhyme and the ditties of no tone over heard melodies, the speaker cooperates in the loss of the voice that should distinguish Keats's art from the pictorial art of the urn.

Keats attempts to overcome this imminent loss by having his speaker talk to the figures on the urn, the fair youth and the bold lover. Crossing the boundary between beholder and object, he animates the frieze, but the triumph of empathy, the consolation he offers the lover, points back to the speaker as well, for the possibility of grief attaches more nearly to the danger of his disappearance within the frieze. The celebration of the love depicted on the urn in the third stanza brings with it the denigration of human passion, a reminder of the "disagreeables" (*Letters* 1: 192) the urn escapes. It seems truer to the dynamics of the poem to see these as a recoil from celebration of the unattainable than to accept them as a final statement about human existence. If this denigration also, in the single word "breathing," reminds us of what human beings do that urns can't, it does so by disrupting the identification between the beholder of the urn and the reader of the poem, reminding us that we are living readers and he is only a figure produced by language.

The fourth stanza marks the point of greatest risk for the beholder of the urn, because the direction implied in his exclamation "who are these coming to the sacrifice?" places him within the frieze. Throughout the poem the effect of motion has been achieved by a series of present participles—"winning," "panting," "breathing," "burning," "parching"—a series that is cut off by "sacrifice": the last present participle of the poem is the "lowing" of the heifer about to be slaughtered. The shift from the passion of the first two stanzas to the stately tableau of the fourth, from the speaker's erotic imaginings to comforting assurances, is fittingly accompanied by another compensation: the appeal to ideas of mystery and priesthood. In the sequence of the poem these terms appear in conjunction with certain ways of placing oneself in relation to the urn. Keats does not depict the urn as a timeless self-enclosed symbol: I suggest that the fourth stanza hints that to apprehend art as if it were self-enclosed is, in the resonant word of the last line, to make oneself into a priest of desolation, to foreclose the possibility of connection with the human world.

By the end of the fourth stanza the two kindred modes of reading suggested by the ode thus far reach a dead end. The conception of the urn as ignoring its audience makes all attempts to know it a ravishing that destroys both other and self. "We hate poetry that has a palpable design on us," Keats declares in a famous criticism of Wordsworth that the class will just have read: "we need not be teazed with grandeur & merit—when we can have them uncontaminated & unobtrusive" (*Letters* 1: 224–25). But perhaps one can also hate poetry that has no design on us, that by making no claim on us leaves us the intolerable choice of self-annihilation or rape.

To develop these strange erotics of reading, I turn to the letters; Keats's experience of Jane Cox, that Charmian with "the Beauty of a Leopardess," shows students that the problems of poetry are not distinct from those of life. "I always find myself more at ease with such a woman," Keats wrote to his brother:

> [T]he picture before me always gives me a life and animation which I cannot possibly feel with any thing inferiour—I am at such times too much occupied in admiring to be awkward or on a tremble. I forget myself entirely because I live in her.

This pose of disinterested spectatorship dissolves in the course of the letter, if indeed it is not already a transparent response to the disturbance set off by Jane Cox's "magnetic Power." Proclaiming that he has "no *sensations*" in regard to Jane Cox and no desire to possess her, Keats confesses feelings precisely the opposite of those that permit him to forget himself. "She kept me awake one Night," he admits, "as a tune of Mozart's might do" (*Letters* 1: 395).

This last comparison moves from the dangers of sight to the pleasures of hearing, transforming Jane Cox's dangerous beauty into intriguing melody. The self-protective sequence is fully articulated in a letter Keats had written to J. H. Reynolds a month earlier:

> [T]he voice and the shape of a woman has haunted me these two days—at such a time when the relief, the feverous relief of Poetry seems a much less crime—This morning Poetry has conquered—I

have relapsed into those abstractions which are my only life—I feel
escaped from a new strange and threatening sorrow. (*Letters* 1: 370)

As with the "Ode on a Grecian Urn" half a year later, the voice and shape
of a sexually charged spectacle haunt Keats, but its resistance to being
grasped proves a burden from which he turns to the "abstractions" of poetry,
a turning that, the letter acknowledges, is a relapse and an escape. Though
he had confidently criticized Wordsworth's didacticism, Keats here confronts
a painful teasing of another sort and repeats the older poet's turn from enigma
to abstraction.

The second mode of reading also collapses at the end of the fourth stanza.
If Keats declares that a "Poet . . . has no Identity—he is continually in
for—and filling some other Body," the effort to fill the silence of the Grecian
urn by inhabiting it betrays the dangers of what even then Keats had seen
as a "wretched" confession inseparable from fears of "an[ni]hilat[ion]" (*Letters* 1: 387). Keats's poem suggests that one cannot be both within the frieze
and outside it, observing: the beholder who enters the circle of representations sacrifices the ongoing life beyond the circle of which the unseen
"little town" is the emblem. Reading, however, would seem to demand
exactly the paradox the poem exposes: readers must animate the text by
their own desires yet remain outside it, retaining their independence by
allowing the text its impenetrable otherness.

Bringing to bear on the ode these foreshadowings from the letters enables
students to understand a configuration central to Keats. The apostrophe "O
Attic shape" with which the fifth stanza begins parallels the only previous
apostrophe in the poem, the "O mysterious priest" of the fourth stanza: as
the urn metamorphoses from the "historian" of the first stanza to the mute
"Attic shape" and pantomimic "Fair attitude" of the last, so too has the
beholder become a voiceless hieratic gesture. The speaker's repudiation of
the urn, the reversal that frees him from this dumb enchantment, is his
dismissal of it as a "Cold Pastoral." The last five lines of the poem move, in
the words of "Sleep and Poetry," from the realm of Flora and old Pan to
the agonies and strife of human hearts. This stanza also recalls the pattern
of the opening stanza with an address to the urn ("Thou" in line 44 as in
lines 1 and 2) but reverses the empathic entering of the scene in stanzas 2
through 4. This new distance between speaker and urn comes as a result of
the speaker's turning from the mystified view of the urn as a symbol to a
recognition of the inevitability of the allegorical mode, a saddened admission
of the imposition of meaning on a blank network of figures. The apothegm
of the urn, "Beauty is truth, truth beauty," is couched in the abstractions
of allegory, self-mirroring and enclosed, and it cannot be incidental that the
only previous instance of the copulative "is" in the poem comes in the phrase
"is emptied."

But such a reading, I try to persuade students, does not resolve the question of where readers are to place themselves in regard to such a deconstruction: that question requires a longer look at the last five lines of the poem. Nothing seems more significant than that the hitherto silent urn should suddenly speak. The crossing from tropes of sight to a trope of voice is crucial—and not only because it reverses addresser and addressee and moves the poem from the exterior world of beholding to the interior world of hearing. The particular generosity of Keats's poem is that whereas the reassertion of voice is the value against which the urn is diminished, voice is attributed as well to the urn: the gesture establishes a dramatic exchange, recovering the lost voice of the speaker by endowing the urn with speech. Students immediately notice that the "speech" is an act of ventriloquism, seemingly little different from the drama projected onto the urn earlier, but a shift in tenses makes clear how we are to take this sleight. The future, "Thou shalt remain," remains in the present tense: "say'st." The urn, as a piece of sculpture, is frozen in the present, a limitation reflected in Keats's static copulatives: "Beauty is truth . . . that is all." Its place in time is the consequence not of its own capacity to tell stories, to enter narrative, but of its transmissibility: the survival of a blank form that can be renewed by a beholder. In Keats's verse the perpetual present is the readers' time, wherein they confront themselves as an audience within the text and as living persons outside it, renewing the poem as the beholder renews the urn.

That "as" returns me to my initial concerns. To encounter oneself through the urn's voice is to encounter one's own death: "When old age shall this generation waste, / Thou shalt remain, in midst of other woe / Than ours, a friend to man, to whom thou say'st. . . ." "[T]his generation" moves readers from the timeless artifact (whether urn or poem) to their own lives: the death Keats invokes here is not only absorption, as earlier in the poem, but the end of life itself. The conclusion of the "Ode on a Grecian Urn," like that of many Romantic poems, is an act of mourning, a relinquishing that is, however, also an opening of the future.

This perspective is the poem's final image of reading, and it explains why the urn can be cherished as a "friend." In *Endymion* Keats places love and friendship together as the "chief intensity," the "Richer entanglements, enthralments far / More self-destroying" (1.800, 798–99). The rapid evolution, or perhaps one should say, involution, of Keats's work after *Endymion* drives love and friendship apart: love in the ode is passion, an *ekstasis* that destroys the distance on which the survival of the self depends. Friendship installs distance: to read is to recognize the text as proceeding from another. The urn's initial silence mimes a refusal to dominate the reader, as Keats scorned Wordsworth's poetry for seeking to do; the reader's acceptance of his distance from the eternity of the text is his refusal to treat reading as an exercise of power or the triumph of desire. (I characterize the reader as male because the parallelism between beholder and reader projects a male reader. Not the least virtue of the poem is its power to make readers aware of the differentials of gender in their own reading experiences.) Keats's model reader chooses the losses from which the lover on the urn is preserved, maintaining the gaps that ensure independence and a continuing life in time. In that silence and division arises Keats's own writing, the rhyme that tells of the beholder's frustration, shuttling between the eternal bliss that is death on the urn and the mortality outside. The several puns in the last stanza, by teasing us to explore two ideas at once, counter our absorption in the poem's images. The claim the poem silently makes on us is perpetually to renew its lifeless saying by acknowledging through it our desires and defeats. The urn thus becomes a friend: what it speaks is all we need to know because it is all we can know on "earth"—a word that occurs more often in Keats's verse than "beauty" and "truth" combined—but we need to prove it, in Keats's phrase, "upon our pulses" (*Letters* 1: 279), by reenacting the experiences of self and loss of self that reading provides.

And yet the power of the poem is to show that the kind of reading this ideal of friendship would make possible remains precarious; the urn's speech is the beholder's fiction, and if he, even in the seemingly self-abnegating gesture of the conclusion, cannot escape transforming the silent urn and its figures into a comforting response to his own yearning, perhaps neither can we in reading Keats's poem. For the urn, beauty is truth, truth beauty; for the reader, teased out of thought by that gnomic utterance, Keats's leaf-fringed legend leaves provocatively unresolved the persistent dilemmas of desire in all our readings, of others, of urns, and of poems.

CONTRIBUTORS AND SURVEY PARTICIPANTS

We wish to thank the following scholars and teachers of Keats who generously participated in the survey and the call for essays that laid the foundation for this volume. Without their invaluable efforts, this volume would not have been possible.

Joan Baum, York College; Harry R. Beaudry, University of Texas, Arlington; Kirk H. Beetz, National University; G. E. Bentley, Jr., University of Toronto; Ernest Bernhardt-Kabisch, Indiana University, Bloomington; Robert Bledsoe, University of Texas, El Paso; Matthew C. Brennan, Indiana State University; David Bromwich, Princeton University; Jewel Spears Brooker, Eckerd College; Teresa M. Brown, University of Florida; Paul A. Cantor, University of Virginia; Bruce Clarke, Texas Tech University; Thomas E. Connolly, State University of New York, Buffalo; Steven N. Craig, Illinois State University; William Crisman, University of California, Berkeley; Marian H. Cusac, Francis Marion College; Mario L. D'Avanzo, Queens College; Hermione de Almeida, University of Miami; Carol E. Dietrich, Ohio State University; Nathaniel Elliott, William and Mary College; David V. Erdman, State University of New York, Stony Brook; Norman Fruman, University of Minnesota, Minneapolis; Robert F. Gleckner, Duke University; Donald C. Goellnicht, McMaster University; Morris Golden, University of Massachusetts, Amherst; Nancy Moore Goslee, University of Tennessee, Knoxville; John E. Grant, University of Iowa; Jean Hall, California State University, Fullerton; John Hayden, University of California, Davis; Wolf Z. Hirst, University of Haifa; David G. Holborn, University of Wisconsin, Stevens Point; Paul G. Italia, Hostos Community College; Mary Lynn Johnson (Grant), University of Iowa; Leonidas M. Jones, University of Vermont; Frank Jordan, Miami University; Edward Kessler, American University; Beth Lau, Ripon College; Barbara Fass Leavy, Queens College; David J. Leigh, S. J., Seattle University; Paul Magnuson, New York University; Bernard J. Mahoney, Houston Community College; Peter Manning, University of Southern California; Edwin W. Marrs, Jr., University of Pittsburgh; Nathalie Marshall-Nadel, Nova University; Richard E. Matlak, Holy Cross College; Fleming McClelland, Northeast Louisiana University; Patricia A. McEahern, University of Colorado, Boulder; Karen E. McGuire, Pasadena City College; Anne K. Mellor, University of California, Los Angeles; Lore Metzger, Emory University; Dan Miller, North Carolina State University; Virgil Nemoianu, Catholic University of America; Marjorie Norris, New York, NY; James O'Rourke, University of Washington; Mark Parker, Randolph-Macon College; Charles I. Patterson, Jr., University of Georgia; Donald Pearce, University of California, Santa Barbara; David Perkins, Harvard University; Stuart Peterfreund, Northeastern University; Vincent F. Petronella, University of Massachusetts, Boston; Mary A. Quinn,

University of San Diego; Tilottama Rajan, University of Western Ontario; Mark Reynolds, Jefferson Davis Junior College; Jeffrey C. Robinson, University of Colorado, Boulder; Clark Rodewald, Bard College; Daniel W. Ross, Allentown College; Molly Rothenberg, Beloit College; Robert M. Ryan, Rutgers University; Ben R. Schneider, Lawrence University; Ronald A. Sharp, Kenyon College; Paul D. Sheats, University of California, Los Angeles; Frederick W. Shilstone, Clemson University; Louise Z. Smith, University of Massachusetts, Boston; Stuart M. Sperry, Indiana University, Bloomington; Jack Stillinger, University of Illinois, Urbana; Patrick Story, George Mason University; Edward Strickland, University of Puerto Rico; Peter Valenti, Fayetteville State University; Leon Waldoff, University of Illinois, Urbana; Aileen Ward, New York University; Nicholas O. Warner, Claremont McKenna College; Daniel P. Watkins, Duquesne University; Brian Wilkie, University of Arkansas, Fayetteville; Susan Wolfson, Rutgers University; Andelys Wood, Union College; Ruth L. Wright, Auburn University.

WORKS CITED
AND RECOMMENDED

Books and Articles

Abrams, M. H. *The Mirror and the Lamp: Romantic Theory and the Critical Tradition.* New York: Oxford UP, 1953.

———. *Natural Supernaturalism: Tradition and Revolution in Romantic Literature.* New York: Norton, 1971.

———, ed. *The Norton Anthology of English Literature.* 5th ed. Vol. 2. New York: Norton, 1986.

———. "Structure and Style in the Greater Romantic Lyric." Hilles 526–60.

Adams, Hazard, ed. *Critical Theory since Plato.* New York: Harcourt, 1971.

Allen, Glen O. "The Fall of Endymion: A Study in Keats's Intellectual Growth." *Keats-Shelley Journal* 6 (1957): 37–57.

Altick, Richard D. *The English Common Reader: A Social History of the Mass Reading Public, 1800–1900.* Chicago: U of Chicago P, 1957.

———. *Paintings from Books: Art and Literature in Britain, 1760–1900.* Columbus: Ohio State UP, 1985.

Anderson, George K., William E. Buckler, and Mary Harris Veeder, eds. *The Literature of England.* 3rd ed. Vol. 2. Glenview: Scott, 1979.

Aske, Martin. *Keats and Hellenism: An Essay.* Cambridge: Cambridge UP, 1985.

Bain, Carl E., et al., eds. *The Norton Introduction to Literature.* 4th ed. New York: Norton, 1986.

Baker, Jeffrey. *John Keats and Symbolism.* New York: St. Martin's, 1986.

Bakhtin, M. M. *Rabelais and His World.* Cambridge: MIT P, 1968.

Baldwin, Edward [William Godwin]. *The Pantheon: Or, Ancient History of the Gods of Greece and Rome.* 1806. 4th ed. London: printed for M. J. Godwin, 1814. New York: Garland, 1984.

Barnard, John. *John Keats.* Cambridge: Cambridge UP, 1987.

Barth, J. Robert. *The Symbolic Imagination: Coleridge and the Romantic Tradition.* Princeton: Princeton UP, 1977.

Barthes, Roland. *Image, Music, Text.* Ed. and trans. Stephen Heath. London: Fontana; New York: Hill, 1977.

———. *S/Z.* 1970. Trans. Richard Miller. New York: Hill; London: Cape, 1977.

Bartholomae, David. "The Study of Error." *College Composition and Communication* 31 (1980): 253–69.

Barzun, Jacques. *Classic, Romantic, and Modern*. Garden City: Doubleday, 1961.

Bate, Walter Jackson. *The Burden of the Past and the English Poet*. Cambridge: Harvard UP, 1970.

———. *From Classic to Romantic: Premises of Taste in Eighteenth-Century England*. Cambridge: Harvard UP, 1946.

———. *John Keats*. 1963. New York: Oxford UP, 1966.

———, ed. *Keats: A Collection of Critical Essays*. Twentieth Century Views. Englewood Cliffs: Spectrum-Prentice, 1964.

———. *The Stylistic Development of Keats*. 1945. New York: Humanities, 1958.

Becker, Michael G., Robert J. Dilligan, and Todd K. Bender, eds. *A Concordance to the Poems of John Keats*. New York: Garland, 1981.

Berthoff, Ann E. *Forming, Thinking, Writing: The Composing Imagination*. Rochelle Park: Hayden, 1978.

Bettelheim, Bruno. *The Uses of Enchantment: The Meaning and Importance of Fairy Tales*. New York: Knopf, 1976.

Blackstone, Bernard. *The Consecrated Urn: An Interpretation of Keats in Terms of Growth and Form*. New York: Longmans, 1959.

Bleich, David. *Subjective Criticism*. Baltimore: Johns Hopkins UP, 1978.

Bloom, Harold. *A Map of Misreading*. New York: Oxford UP, 1975.

———, ed. *The Odes of Keats*. New York: Chelsea, 1987.

———. *Poetry and Repression: Revisionism from Blake to Stevens*. New Haven: Yale UP, 1976.

———, ed. *Romanticism and Consciousness: Essays in Criticism*. New York: Norton, 1970.

———. *The Visionary Company: A Reading of English Romantic Poetry*. 1961. Ithaca: Cornell UP, 1971.

Bloom, Harold, and Lionel Trilling, eds. *Romantic Poetry and Prose*. New York: Oxford UP, 1973. Vol. 4 of *The Oxford Anthology of English Literature*. 6 vols.

Bonnycastle, John. *An Introduction to Astronomy*. 5th ed. London: Johnson, 1807.

Booth, Wayne C. "Reply to Richard Berrong." *Critical Inquiry* 11.4 (1985): 697–701.

———. *The Rhetoric of Fiction*. Chicago: U of Chicago P, 1961.

Bostetter, Edward E. *The Romantic Ventriloquists: Wordsworth, Coleridge, Keats, Shelley, Byron*. Seattle: U of Washington P, 1963.

Bowra, Cecil M. *The Romantic Imagination*. 1949. London: Oxford UP, 1984.

Bridges, Robert. *John Keats, A Critical Essay*. London: privately printed, 1895.

Briggs, Asa. *The Making of Modern England: 1783–1867*. New York: Harper, 1965.

Briggs, Harold E. "Keats, Robertson, and *That Most Hateful Land*." *PMLA* 59 (1944): 184–99.

Brooks, Cleanth. "History without Footnotes: An Account of Keats' Urn." *Sewanee Review* 52 (1944): 89–101. Rpt. as "Keats's Sylvan Historian: History without Footnotes." *The Well-Wrought Urn: Studies in the Structure of Poetry.* By Brooks. 1947. New York: Harcourt, 1975. 139–52.

Brooks, Cleanth, and Robert Penn Warren, eds. *Understanding Poetry.* 1938. 4th ed. New York: Holt, 1976.

Brown, Charles Armitage. *The Letters of Charles Armitage Brown.* Ed. Jack Stillinger. Cambridge: Harvard UP, 1966.

———. *Life of John Keats by Charles Armitage Brown.* Ed. Dorothy Hyde Bodurtha and Willard Bissell Pope. London: Oxford UP, 1937.

Burnet, Gilbert. *History of His Own Time.* London, 1809.

Burton, Robert. *The Anatomy of Melancholy. . . .* 1621. Ed. Holbrook Jackson. London: Dent, 1977.

Bush, Douglas. *John Keats: His Life and Writings.* 1966. New York: Collier, 1967.

———. *Mythology and the Renaissance Tradition in English Poetry.* 1932. Rev. ed. New York: Norton, 1963.

———. *Mythology and the Romantic Tradition in English Poetry.* 1937. New York: Norton, 1969.

Butler, Marilyn. *Romantics, Rebels, and Reactionaries: English Literature and Its Background, 1760–1830.* New York: Oxford UP, 1981.

Caldwell, James Ralston. *John Keats' Fancy: The Effect on Keats of the Psychology of His Day.* 1945. New York: Octagon, 1965.

Chatterjee, Bhabatosh. *John Keats: His Mind and Work.* New Delhi: Orient Longman, 1971.

Chayes, Irene H. "Dreamer, Poet, and Poem in 'The Fall of Hyperion.' " *Philological Quarterly* 46 (1967): 499–515.

Child, Francis James. *The English and Scottish Popular Ballads.* 1884. 5 vols. New York: Pageant, 1956.

Clarke, Charles Cowden, and Mary Cowden Clarke. *Recollections of Writers.* 1878. Ed. Robert Gittings. Fontwell, Eng.: Centaur, 1969.

Clubbe, John, and Ernest J. Lovell, Jr. *English Romanticism: The Grounds of Belief.* DeKalb: Northern Illinois UP, 1983.

Cohen, Jane Rabb. "Keats's Humor in 'La Belle Dame sans Merci.' " *Keats-Shelley Journal* 17 (1968): 10–13.

Colvin, Sidney. *John Keats: His Life and Poetry, His Friends, Critics, and After-Fame.* 1917. New York: Octagon, 1970.

Cooke, Michael G. *Acts of Inclusion: Studies Bearing on an Elementary Theory of Romanticism.* New Haven: Yale UP, 1979.

Crews, Frederick. *The Pooh Perplex: A Freshman Casebook.* New York: Dutton, 1963.

Curran, Stuart. *Poetic Form and British Romanticism*. New York: Oxford UP, 1986.

Cusac, Marian Hollingsworth. "Keats as Enchanter: An Organizing Principle of 'The Eve of St. Agnes.' " *Keats-Shelley Journal* 17 (1968): 113–19.

Dante Alighieri. *The Divine Comedy*. Trans. H. R. Huse. New York: Holt, 1954.

Danzig, Alan, ed. *Twentieth-Century Interpretations of "The Eve of St. Agnes": A Collection of Critical Essays*. Twentieth Century Interpretations. Englewood Cliffs: Spectrum-Prentice, 1971.

D'Avanzo, Mario L. *Keats's Metaphors for the Poetic Imagination*. Durham: Duke UP, 1967.

de Man, Paul. *Allegories of Reading: Figural Language in Rousseau, Nietzsche, Rilke, and Proust*. New Haven: Yale UP, 1979.

———. Introduction. *John Keats: Selected Poetry*. Ed. de Man. ix–xxxvi.

———. "Keats and Hölderlin." *Comparative Literature* 8 (1956): 28–45.

De Quincey, Thomas. *De Quincey as Critic*. Ed. John E. Jordan. London: Routledge, 1973.

Dickstein, Morris. *Keats and His Poetry: A Study in Development*. Chicago: Chicago UP, 1971.

Doctorow, E. L. *Lives of the Poets: Six Stories and a Novella*. New York: Random, 1984.

Dussler, Luitpold. *Raphael: A Critical Catalogue of His Pictures, Wall-Paintings, and Tapestries*. Trans. Sebastian Cruft. London: Phaidon, 1971.

Eaves, Morris, and Michael Fischer. *Romanticism and Contemporary Criticism*. Ithaca: Cornell UP, 1986.

Eco, Umberto. "The Poetics of the Open Work." *The Role of the Reader: Explorations in the Semiotics of Texts*. By Eco. Bloomington: Indiana UP, 1979. 47–66.

Edie, James M., ed. *The Primacy of Perception and Other Essays on Phenomenological Psychology, the Philosophy of Art, History, and Politics*. Evanston: Northwestern UP, 1964.

Eichner, Hans. "The Rise of Modern Science and the Genesis of Romanticism." *PMLA* 97 (1982): 8–30.

Elkins, A. C., Jr., and L. J. Forstner, eds. *The Romantic Movement Bibliography, 1936–1970: A Master Cumulation from ELH, Philological Quarterly, and English Language Notes*. 7 vols. Ann Arbor: Pierian, 1973.

Ellis, Helen B. "Food, Sex, Death, and the Feminine Principle in Keats's Poetry." *English Studies in Canada* 6 (1980): 56–74.

Elton, Oliver. *A Survey of English Literature, 1780–1830*. London: Arnold, 1912. Vol. 1 of *A Survey of English Literature, 1780–1880*. 2 vols. 1912–20.

Ende, Stuart A. *Keats and the Sublime*. New Haven: Yale UP, 1976.

Engell, James. *The Creative Imagination: Enlightenment to Romanticism*. Cambridge: Harvard UP, 1981.

Enscoe, Gerald. *Eros and the Romantics: Sexual Love as a Theme in Coleridge, Shelley, and Keats*. The Hague: Mouton, 1967.

Everett, Barbara. "Keats: Somebody Reading." *Poets in Their Time: Essays on English Poetry from Donne to Larkin.* By Everett. London: Faber, 1986. 140–58.

Evert, Walter H. *Aesthetic and Myth in the Poetry of Keats.* Princeton: Princeton UP, 1965.

Fass, Barbara. *"La Belle Dame sans Merci" and the Aesthetics of Romanticism.* Detroit: Wayne State UP, 1974.

Finney, Claude Lee. *The Evolution of Keats's Poetry.* 2 vols. Cambridge: Harvard UP, 1936.

Fish, Stanley. *Is There a Text in This Class? The Authority of Interpretive Communities.* Cambridge: Harvard UP, 1980.

Flick, A. J. "Keats's First Reading of Dante's *Divine Comedy.*" *Notes and Queries* ns 25 (1978): 225.

Fogle, Richard Harter. *The Imagery of Keats and Shelley: A Comparative Study.* 1949. Hamden: Archon, 1962.

———, ed. *Romantic Poets and Prose Writers.* Goldentree Bibliographies in Language and Literature. Northbrook: AHM, 1967.

Ford, George H. *Keats and the Victorians.* New Haven: Yale UP, 1944.

Ford, Newell F. *The Prefigurative Imagination of John Keats: A Study of the Beauty-Truth Identification and Its Implications.* 1951. Hamden: Archon, 1966.

Foucault, Michel. *Power/Knowledge: Selected Interviews and Other Writings, 1972–1977.* Ed. Colin Gordon. New York: Pantheon, 1980.

Freeman, Donald. "Keats's 'To Autumn': Poetry as Process and Pattern." *Language and Style* 11 (1978): 3–17.

Fry, Paul H. "History, Existence, and 'To Autumn.' " *Studies in Romanticism* 25 (1986): 211–19.

Frye, Northrop. *Anatomy of Criticism: Four Essays.* Princeton: Princeton UP, 1957.

———. "The Drunken Boat: The Revolutionary Element in Romanticism." Frye, *Romanticism Reconsidered.* 1–25.

———, ed. *Romanticism Reconsidered: Selected Papers from the English Institute.* New York: Columbia UP, 1963.

———. *A Study of English Romanticism.* 1968. Chicago: Chicago UP, 1982.

Furst, Lilian, R. *Fictions of Romantic Irony in European Narrative, 1760–1857.* London: Macmillan, 1984.

———. *European Romanticism: Self-Definition.* London: Methuen, 1980.

———. *Romanticism.* 1969. 2nd ed. London: Methuen, 1976.

———. *Romanticism in Perspective.* London: Macmillan, 1969.

Garrod, H. W. *Keats.* 1926. Oxford: Clarendon, 1967.

Gaull, Marilyn. *English Romanticism: The Human Context.* New York: Norton, 1988.

Gittings, Robert. *John Keats.* Boston: Little, 1968.

———. *John Keats: The Living Year, 21 September 1818 to 21 September 1819.* 1954. New York: Barnes, 1968.

———. *The Mask of Keats: A Study of Problems.* Cambridge: Harvard UP, 1956.

Gleckner, Robert F., and Gerald E. Enscoe, eds. *Romanticism: Points of View.* 1962. Detroit: Wayne State UP, 1970.

Godfrey, Clarice. *"Endymion."* Muir 20–39.

Godwin, William. *See* Baldwin, Edward.

Goellnicht, Donald C. "Keats on Reading: 'Delicious Diligent Indolence.' " *Journal of English and Germanic Philology* 88 (1989): 190–210.

———. *The Poet-Physician: Keats and Medical Science.* Pittsburgh: U of Pittsburgh P, 1984.

Goldberg, M. A. *The Poetics of Romanticism: Toward a Reading of John Keats.* Yellow Springs: Antioch UP, 1969.

Goslee, Nancy Moore. "Phidian Lore: Sculpture and Personification in Keats's Odes." *Studies in Romanticism* 21 (1982): 73–86.

———. " 'Under a Cloud in Prospect': Keats, Milton, and Stationing." *Philological Quarterly* 53 (1974): 205–19.

———. *Uriel's Eye: Miltonic Stationing and Statuary in Blake, Keats, and Shelley.* University: U of Alabama P, 1985.

Gradman, Barry. *Metamorphosis in Keats.* New York: New York UP, 1980.

Graves, Robert. *The White Goddess: A Historical Grammar of Poetic Myth.* Amended and enl. ed. New York: Vintage, 1958.

Green, David Bonnell, and Edwin Graves Wilson, eds. *Keats, Shelley, Byron, Hunt, and Their Circles: A Bibliography: July 1, 1950–June 30, 1962.* Lincoln: U of Nebraska P, 1964.

Hagstrum, Jean H. *The Romantic Body: Love and Sexuality in Keats, Wordsworth, and Blake.* Knoxville: U of Tennessee P, 1985.

———. *The Sister Arts: The Tradition of Literary Pictorialism and English Poetry from Dryden to Gray.* Chicago: U of Chicago P, 1958.

Halévy, Élie. *England in 1815.* Trans. E. I. Watkin and D. A. Barker. 1949. New York: Barnes, 1968.

Harding, Anthony John. "Speech, Silence, and the Self-Doubting Interpreter in Keats's Poetry." *Keats-Shelley Journal* 35 (1986): 83–103.

Harrison, Robert. "Symbolism of the Cyclical Myth in *Endymion.*" *Texas Studies in Literature and Language* 1 (1960): 538–54.

Hartley, Robert A., ed. *Keats, Shelley, Byron, Hunt, and Their Circles: A Bibliography: July 1, 1962–December 31, 1974.* Lincoln: U of Nebraska P, 1978.

Hartman, Geoffrey. "Beyond Formalism." *MLN* 81 (1966): 542–57. Rpt. in *Beyond Formalism: Literary Essays, 1958–1970.* By Hartman. New Haven: Yale UP, 1970. 42–57.

———. "Poem and Ideology: A Study of Keats's 'To Autumn.' " *Literary Theory and Structure: Essays in Honor of William K. Wimsatt.* Ed. Frank Brady, John Palmer, and Martin Price. New Haven: Yale UP, 1973. 305–30.

———. "Spectral Symbolism and the Authorial Self: An Approach to Keats's 'Hyperion.' " *Essays in Criticism* 24 (1974): 1–19.

Harvey, A. D. *English Poetry in a Changing Society, 1780–1825.* New York: St. Martin's, 1980.

Havens, Raymond Dexter. *The Influence of Milton on English Poetry.* 1922. New York: Russell, 1961.

Haydon, Benjamin Robert. *The Diary of Benjamin Robert Haydon.* Ed. Willard Bissell Pope. 5 vols. Cambridge: Harvard UP, 1960–63.

Hearn, Ronald B., et al., eds. *Keats Criticism since 1954: A Bibliography.* Romantic Reassessment 83.3. Salzburg: Institut für Anglistik und Amerikanistik, Universität Salzburg, 1981.

Heath, William, ed. *Major British Poets of the Romantic Period.* New York: Macmillan, 1973.

Hegel, G. W. F. *Aesthetics: Lectures on Fine Art.* Trans. T. M. Knox. 2 vols. Oxford: Clarendon, 1975.

Hepworth, Brian, ed. *The Rise of Romanticism: Essential Texts.* Manchester, Eng.: Carcanet, 1978.

Hewlett, Dorothy. *A Life of John Keats.* 1937. 2nd ed. Rev. and enl. New York: Barnes, 1950.

Hilles, Frederick W., and Harold Bloom, eds. *From Sensibility to Romanticism: Essays Presented to Frederick A. Pottle.* New York: Oxford UP, 1965.

Hilton, Timothy. *Keats and His World.* New York: Viking, 1971.

Hinden, Michael. "Reading the Painting, Seeing the Poem: Vermeer and Keats." *Mosaic* 17 (1984): 17–34.

Hirst, Wolf Z. *John Keats.* Twayne's English Authors Series 334. Boston: Twayne, 1981.

Holland, Norman N. *Five Readers Reading.* New Haven: Yale UP, 1975.

Holman, C. Hugh. *A Handbook to Literature.* 1972. 3rd ed. Indianapolis: Bobbs, 1978.

Homans, Margaret. "Keats Reading Women, Women Reading Keats." *Studies in Romanticism* 29 (1990): 341–70.

Honour, Hugh. *Romanticism.* New York: Harper, 1979.

Houghton, Lord [Richard Monckton Milnes]. *Life, Letters, and Literary Remains of John Keats.* 2 vols. London: Moxon, 1848.

Hungerford, Edward B. *Shores of Darkness.* New York: Columbia UP, 1941.

Hunt, Leigh. *The Autobiography of Leigh Hunt.* Ed. J. E. Morpurgo. London: Cresset, 1948.

Iser, Wolfgang. "The Reading Process: A Phenomenological Approach." *The Implied Reader: Patterns of Communication in Prose Fiction from Bunyan to Beckett.* By Iser. Baltimore: Johns Hopkins UP, 1974. 274–94.

Jack, Ian. *English Literature, 1815–1832.* New York: Oxford UP, 1963. Vol. 10 of *The Oxford History of English Literature.* 13 vols. 1945–86.

———. *Keats and the Mirror of Art.* 1967. Oxford: Clarendon, 1968.

Jackson, J. R. de J. *Poetry of the Romantic Period.* London: Routledge, 1984. Vol. 4 of *Routledge History of English Poetry.* 7 vols. 1977–81.

James, D. G. *The Romantic Comedy*. New York: Oxford UP, 1948.

Jauss, Hans Robert. "The Poetic Text within the Change of Horizons of Reading: The Example of Baudelaire's 'Spleen II.' " *Toward an Aesthetic of Reception*. By Jauss. Trans. Timothy Bahti. Minneapolis: U of Minnesota P, 1982. 139–85.

Johnston, Arthur. *Enchanted Ground: The Study of Medieval Romance in the Eighteenth Century*. London: Athlone, 1964.

Jones, James Land. *Adam's Dream: Mythic Consciousness in Keats and Yeats*. Athens: U of Georgia P, 1975.

Jones, John. *John Keats's Dream of Truth*. 1969. London: Chatto, 1980.

Jones, Roger, and Nicholas Penny. *Raphael*. New Haven: Yale UP, 1983.

Jordan, Frank, Jr., ed. *The English Romantic Poets: A Review of Research and Criticism*. 3rd ed. 1972. 4th ed. New York: MLA, 1985.

Kaplan, Charles. *The Overwrought Urn: A Potpourri of Parodies of Critics Who Triumphantly Present the Real Meaning of Authors from Jane Austen to J. D. Salinger*. New York: Pegasus, 1969.

Kauvar, Gerald B. *The Other Poetry of Keats*. Rutherford: Fairleigh Dickinson UP, 1969.

Keats, John. *The Essential Keats*. Ed. Philip Levine. New York: Ecco, 1987.

———. *John Keats: The Complete Poems*. Ed. John Barnard. Penguin English Poets. 1973. New York: Penguin, 1977.

———. *John Keats: Complete Poems*. Ed. Jack Stillinger. Student's ed. Cambridge: Belknap–Harvard UP, 1982.

———. *John Keats: Complete Poems and Selected Letters*. Ed. Clarence DeWitt Thorpe. New York: Odyssey, 1935.

———. *John Keats: Selected Poems*. Ed. George H. Ford. Northbrook: AHM, 1950.

———. *John Keats: Selected Poems and Letters*. Ed. Douglas Bush. Riverside Editions. Boston: Houghton, 1959.

———. *John Keats: Selected Poetry*. Ed. Paul de Man. Signet Classic Poetry Series. New York: NAL, 1966.

———. *The Letters of John Keats, 1814–1821*. Ed. Hyder Edward Rollins. 2 vols. Cambridge: Harvard UP, 1958.

———. *Letters of John Keats: A New Selection*. Ed. Robert Gittings. 1970. Oxford: Oxford UP, 1979.

———. *The Poems of John Keats*. Ed. Miriam Allott. Annotated English Poets Series. New York: Longman-Norton, 1970.

———. *The Poems of John Keats*. Ed. Ernest De Selincourt. 1905. 5th ed. 1926. London: Methuen, 1951.

———. *The Poems of John Keats*. Ed. Jack Stillinger. Cambridge: Belknap–Harvard UP, 1978.

———. *Poetical Works of John Keats*. Ed. H. W. Garrod. 1939. 2nd ed. 1958. Oxford: Oxford UP, 1978.

————. *The Poetical Works and Other Writings of John Keats.* Ed. H. Buxton Forman and Maurice Buxton Forman. 8 vols. New York: Scribner's, 1938–39.

Kelley, Theresa M. "Poetics and the Politics of Reception: Keats's 'La Belle Dame sans Merci.'" *ELH* 54 (1987): 333–62.

Kern, Robert. "Keats and the Problem of Romance." *Philological Quarterly* 58 (1979): 171–91.

Klancher, Jon. *The Making of English Reading Audiences, 1790–1832.* Madison: U of Wisconsin P, 1987.

————. "Reading the Social Text: Power, Signs, and Audience in Early Nineteenth-Century Prose." *Studies in Romanticism* 23 (1984): 183–204.

Kneale, J. Douglas. "Wordsworth and Milton." *Approaches to Teaching Wordsworth's Poetry.* Ed. Spencer Hall with Jonathan Ramsey. New York: MLA, 1986. 119–23.

Knight, G. Wilson. *The Starlit Dome: Studies in the Poetry of Vision.* 1941. London: Methuen, 1959.

Krieger, Murray. *The Play and Place of Criticism.* Baltimore: Johns Hopkins UP, 1967.

Kroeber, Karl, ed. *Backgrounds to British Romantic Literature.* San Francisco: Chandler, 1968.

————. *British Romantic Art.* Berkeley: U of California P, 1986.

————. "Romantic Historicism: The Temporal Sublime." *Images of Romanticism: Verbal and Visual Affinities.* Ed. Kroeber and William Walling. New Haven: Yale UP, 1978. 149–65.

————. *Romantic Narrative Art.* Madison: U of Wisconsin P, 1966.

Kübler-Ross, Elizabeth. *On Death and Dying.* New York: Macmillan, 1969.

————. *Questions and Answers on Death and Dying.* New York: Macmillan, 1974.

Langbaum, Robert. *The Poetry of Experience: The Dramatic Monologue in Modern Literary Tradition.* New York: Random, 1957.

Larkin, David, ed. *The English Dreamers.* New York: Peacock-Bantam, 1975.

Lau, Beth. "Keats's Mature Goddesses." *Philological Quarterly* 63 (1984): 323–41.

————. "Madeline at Northanger Abbey: Keats's Anti-Romances and Gothic Satire." *Journal of English and Germanic Philology* 84 (1985): 30–50.

Le Comte, Edward S. *Endymion in England: The Literary History of a Greek Myth.* Morningside Heights: King's Crown, 1944.

Lemprière, John. *Bibliotheca Classica: Or, A Classical Dictionary.* 1788. New York: Garland, 1984.

Levinson, Marjorie. *Keats's Life of Allegory: The Origins of a Style.* Oxford: Blackwell, 1988.

Little, Judy. *Keats as a Narrative Poet: A Test of Invention.* Lincoln: U of Nebraska P, 1975.

Lovejoy, A. O. *The Great Chain of Being: A Study of the History of an Idea.* The

William James Lectures Delivered at Harvard University, 1933. 1936. Cambridge: Harvard UP, 1966.

———. "On the Discrimination of Romanticisms." *PMLA* 39 (1924): 229–53. Rpt. in *Essays in the History of Ideas.* By Lovejoy. Baltimore: Johns Hopkins UP, 1948. 228–53.

Low, Donald A. *That Sunny Dome: A Portrait of Regency England.* Totowa: Rowman, 1977.

Lowell, Amy. *John Keats.* 2 vols. Boston: Houghton, 1925.

Lyon, Harvey T., ed. *Keats' Well-Read Urn.* New York: Holt, 1958.

MacGillivray, J. R., ed. *Keats: A Bibliography and Reference Guide with an Essay on Keats' Reputation.* Toronto: U of Toronto P, 1949.

Mahoney, John L., ed. *The English Romantics: Major Poetry and Critical Theory.* Lexington: Heath, 1978.

Marquess, William Henry. *Lives of the Poet: The First Century of Keats Biography.* University Park: Pennsylvania State UP, 1985.

Matthews, G. M., ed. *Keats: The Critical Heritage.* The Critical Heritage Series. New York: Barnes, 1971.

Matthey, François. *The Evolution of Keats's Structural Imagery.* Berne: Franke, 1974.

McGann, Jerome. *The Beauty of Inflections: Literary Investigations in Historical Method and Theory.* Oxford: Clarendon, 1985.

———. "Keats and the Historical Method in Literary Criticism." *MLN* 94 (1979): 988–1032. Rpt. in McGann, *Beauty* 15–65.

———. *The Romantic Ideology: A Critical Investigation.* Chicago: U of Chicago P, 1983.

Mellor, Anne K. *English Romantic Irony.* Cambridge: Harvard UP, 1980.

———. "Keats's Face of Moneta: Source and Meaning." *Keats-Shelley Journal* 25 (1976): 65–80.

———, ed. *Romanticism and Feminism.* Bloomington: Indiana UP, 1987.

Merleau-Ponty, Maurice. *Phenomenology of Perception.* Trans. Colin Smith. Atlantic Highlands: Humanities, 1981.

Metzger, Lore. *One Foot in Eden: Modes of Pastoral in Romantic Poetry.* Chapel Hill: U of North Carolina P, 1986.

Midzunoe, Yuichi. *Sapience: The Philosophy of John Keats.* Tokyo: Shohakusha, 1978.

Milnes, Richard Monckton. *See* Houghton, Lord.

Milton, John. *The Complete Poetical Works of John Milton.* Ed. Douglas Bush. Boston: Houghton, 1965.

Mitchell, W. J. T. *Iconology: Image, Text, Ideology.* Chicago: U of Chicago P, 1986.

Muir, Kenneth, ed. *John Keats: A Reassessment.* 1958. Liverpool: Liverpool UP, 1969.

Murry, John Middleton. *Keats*. 4th ed. New York: Noonday, 1955.

———. *Keats and Shakespeare: A Study of Keats' Poetic Life from 1816 to 1820*. London: Milford, 1925.

Nietzsche, Friedrich Wilhelm. *The Birth of Tragedy and The Genealogy of Morals*. Trans. Francis Golffing. New York: Doubleday, 1956.

O'Neill, Judith, ed. *Critics on Keats: Readings in Literary Criticism*. Coral Gables: U of Miami P, 1968.

Ortner, Sherry B. "Is Female to Male as Nature Is to Culture?" *Woman, Culture, and Society*. Ed. Michelle Zimbalist Rosaldo and Louise Lamphere. Stanford: Stanford UP, 1974. 67–87.

Osgood, Charles Grovesnor. *A Concordance to the Poems of Edmund Spenser*. Washington: Carnegie Institution, 1915. Gloucester: Smith, 1963.

Owen, Frances Mary. *John Keats: A Study*. London: C. Kegan Paul, 1880.

Oxford English Dictionary. Compact ed. Oxford: Oxford UP, 1981.

Parker, Patricia A. *Inescapable Romance: Studies in the Poetics of a Mode*. Princeton: Princeton UP, 1979.

Paton, Lucy A. *Studies in the Fairy Mythology of Arthurian Romance*. 2nd ed. New York: Franklin, 1960.

Patterson, Annabel M. " 'How to load and . . . bend': Syntax and Interpretation in Keats's 'To Autumn.' " *PMLA* 94 (1979): 449–58.

Patterson, Charles I., Jr. *The Daemonic in the Poetry of John Keats*. Urbana: U of Illinois P, 1970.

———. "The Monomyth in the Structure of Keats's *Endymion*." *Keats-Shelley Journal* 31 (1982): 64–81.

Peckham, Morse. *Beyond the Tragic Vision: The Quest for Identity in the Nineteenth Century*. New York: Braziller, 1962.

———. "Toward a Theory of Romanticism." *PMLA* 66 (1951): 5–23.

———. "Toward a Theory of Romanticism II: Reconsiderations." *Studies in Romanticism* 1 (1961): 1–8.

———. *The Triumph of Romanticism: Collected Essays*. Columbia: U of South Carolina P, 1970.

Perkin, Harold James. *The Origins of Modern English Society, 1780–1880*. London: Routledge, 1969.

Perkins, David, ed. *English Romantic Writers*. New York: Harcourt, 1967.

———. "Lamia." Bate, *Keats: A Collection* 143–54.

———. *The Quest for Permanence: The Symbolism of Wordsworth, Shelley, and Keats*. 1959. Cambridge: Harvard UP, 1969.

Peterfreund, Stuart. "Keats and the Fate of the Genres: The Troublesome Middle Term." *Genre* 16 (1983): 249–77.

Pettet, E. C. *On the Poetry of Keats*. 1957. Cambridge: Cambridge UP, 1970.

Pezzini, Grazia Bernini, et al. *Raphael Invenit*. Roma: Quasar, 1985.

Ponsot, Marie, and Rosemary Deen. *Beat Not the Poor Desk*. Upper Montclair: Boynton, 1982.

Potter, John. *Archaeologia Graeca*. 1697, 1699. London, 1804. Edinburgh, 1813, 1814.

Praz, Mario. *The Romantic Agony*. Trans. Angus Davidson. 1933. London: Oxford UP, 1970.

Price, Martin. *To the Palace of Wisdom: Studies in Order and Energy from Dryden to Blake*. 1964. Garden City: Doubleday, 1970.

Prickett, Stephen, ed. *The Romantics*. New York: Holmes, 1981.

Primeau, Ronald. "Chaucer's *Troilus and Criseyde* and Rhythm of Experience in Keats's 'What can I do to drive away.' " *Keats-Shelley Journal* 23 (1974): 106–18.

Princeton Encyclopedia of Poetry and Poetics. Ed. Alex Preminger, with assoc. eds. Frank J. Warnke and O. B. Hardison. 1965. Enl. ed. Princeton: Princeton UP, 1974.

Ragussis, Michael. "Narrative Structure and the Problem of the Divided Reader in 'The Eve of St. Agnes.' " *ELH* 42 (1975): 378–94.

———. *The Subterfuge of Art: Language and the Romantic Tradition*. Baltimore: John Hopkins UP, 1978.

Rajan, Tilottama. *Dark Interpreter: The Discourse of Romanticism*. Ithaca: Cornell UP, 1980.

———. "The Supplement of Reading." *New Literary History* 17.3 (1986): 573–94.

Reiman, Donald H., ed. *English Romantic Poetry, 1800–1835: A Guide to Information Sources*. Detroit: Gale, 1979.

———. *Intervals of Inspiration: The Skeptical Tradition and the Psychology of Romanticism*. Greenwood: Penkevill, 1988.

———, ed. *Shelley, Keats, and London Radical Writers*. New York: Garland, 1972. Part C (vols. 8–9) of *The Romantics Reviewed: Contemporary Reviews of British Romantic Writers*. 9 vols. 1972.

Renwick, William L. *English Literature, 1789–1815*. New York: Oxford UP, 1963. Vol. 9 of *The Oxford History of English Literature*. 13 vols. 1945–86.

Reynolds, John Hamilton. *The Letters of John Hamilton Reynolds*. Ed. Leonidas M. Jones. Lincoln: U of Nebraska P, 1973.

Rhodes, Jack Wright. *Keats's Major Odes: An Annotated Bibliography of the Criticism*. Westport: Greenwood, 1984.

Richards, I. A. *The Philosophy of Rhetoric*. New York: Oxford UP, 1936.

Ricks, Christopher. *Keats and Embarrassment*. Oxford: Clarendon, 1974.

Ridley, M. R. *Keats' Craftsmanship: A Study in Poetic Development*. Oxford: Clarendon, 1933.

Riffaterre, Michael. "Describing Poetic Structures: Two Approaches to Baudelaire's 'Les chats.' " *Yale French Studies* 36–37 (1966): 200–42.

Robertson, William. *The History of America*. 2 vols. London: Strahan, 1777.

————. *The History of Scotland during the Reigns of Queen Mary and of King James VI till His Accession to the Crown of England.* 2 vols. 1759.

Robinson, Dwight E. "Ode on a 'New Etrurian' Urn: A Reflection of Wedgwood Ware in the Poetic Imagery of John Keats." *Keats-Shelley Journal* 12 (1963): 11–35.

Rollins, Hyder Edward, ed. *The Keats Circle: Letters and Papers and More Letters and Poems of the Keats Circle.* 1948. 2nd ed. 2 vols. Cambridge: Harvard UP, 1965.

Rothlisberger, Marcel. *Claude Lorrain: The Paintings.* 1961. New York: Hacker, 1979.

Ryan, Robert M. *Keats: The Religious Sense.* Princeton: Princeton UP, 1976.

Rzepka, Charles J. *Self as Mind: Vision and Identity in Wordsworth, Coleridge, and Keats.* Cambridge: Harvard UP, 1986.

Saly, John. "Keats's Answer to Dante: 'The Fall of Hyperion.' " *Keats-Shelley Journal* 14 (1965): 65–78.

Sandys, George. *Ovid's* Metamorphosis *Englished, Mythologized, and Represented in Figures.* 1632. Ed. Karl K. Hulley and Stanley T. Vandersall. Lincoln: U of Nebraska P, 1970.

Schapiro, Barbara A. *The Romantic Mother: Narcissistic Patterns in Romantic Poetry.* Baltimore: Johns Hopkins UP, 1983.

Schiller, Friedrich. *Naive and Sentimental Poetry.* Naive and Sentimental Poetry *and* On the Sublime. Trans. Julius A. Elias. New York: Ungar, 1966. 81–190.

Sharp, Ronald A. *Keats, Skepticism, and the Religion of Beauty.* Athens: U of Georgia P, 1979.

Sharp, William. *The Life and Letters of Joseph Severn.* New York: Scribner's, 1892.

Sheats, Paul D. "Keats's Second 'Hyperion,' and the 'Purgatorio': Further Notes." *Notes and Queries* ns 15 (1968): 336–38.

Sherwin, Paul. "Dying into Life: Keats's Struggle with Milton in 'Hyperion.' " *PMLA* 93 (1978): 383–95. Rpt. in *Modern Critical Views: John Keats.* Ed. Harold Bloom. New York: Chelsea, 1985. 127–46.

Simpson, David. *Irony and Authority in Romantic Poetry.* Totowa: Rowman, 1979.

————. "Keats's Lady, Metaphor, and the Rhetoric of Neurosis." *Studies in Romanticism* 15 (1976): 265–88.

Slote, Bernice. "The Climate of Keats's 'La Belle Dame sans Merci.' " *Modern Language Quarterly* 21 (1960): 195–207.

————. *Keats and the Dramatic Principle.* Lincoln: U of Nebraska P, 1958.

————. "La Belle Dame as Naiad." *Journal of English and Germanic Philology* 60 (1961): 22–30.

Smith, Louise Z. "Enigma Variations: Reading and Writing through Metaphor." *Only Connect: Uniting Reading and Writing.* Ed. Thomas Newkirk. Upper Montclair: Boynton, 1986. 158–73.

————. "The Material Sublime: Keats and 'Isabella.' " *Studies in Romanticism* 13 (1974): 299–311. Rpt. in *Keats: Narrative Poems*. Ed. John Spencer Hill. London: Macmillan, 1983. 105–18.

Spence, Joseph. *Polymetis: Or, An Enquiry concerning the Agreement between the Works of the Roman Poets and the Remains of the Antient Artists. . . . 1747.* New York: Garland, 1976.

Sperry, Stuart M. *Keats the Poet*. Princeton: Princeton UP, 1973.

————. "Romance as Wish-Fulfillment: 'The Eve of St. Agnes.' " Sperry 198–220.

Steiner, Wendy. *The Colors of Rhetoric: Problems in the Relation between Modern Literature and Painting*. Chicago: U of Chicago P, 1982.

————. *Pictures of Romance: Form against Context in Painting and Literature*. Chicago: U of Chicago P, 1988.

Stephenson, William C. "The Performing Narrator in Keats's Poetry." *Keats-Shelley Journal* 26 (1977): 51–71.

Stevens, Wallace. *The Palm at the End of the Mind: Selected Poems and a Play by Wallace Stevens*. Ed. Holly Stevens. 1971. New York: Random, 1972.

Stewart, Garrett. " 'Lamia' and the Language of Metamorphosis." *Studies in Romanticism* 15 (1976): 3–41.

Stillinger, Jack. *The Hoodwinking of Madeline and Other Essays on Keats's Poems*. Urbana: U of Illinois P, 1971.

————. "The Hoodwinking of Madeline: Skepticism in 'The Eve of St. Agnes.' " Stillinger, *Hoodwinking* 67–93.

————, ed. "John Keats." Abrams, *Norton Anthology* 793–877.

————. "Keats and Romance." *Studies in English Literature* 8 (1968): 593–605.

————, ed. Vol. 1: [Keats's] Poems *(1817): A Facsimile of Richard Woodhouse's Annotated Copy in the Huntington Library*; vol. 2: Endymion: *A Facsimile of the Revised Holograph Manuscript*; vol. 3: Endymion *(1818): A Facsimile of Richard Woodhouse's Annotated Copy in the Berg Collection*; vol. 4: [Keats's] *Poems, Transcripts, Letters, etc.: Facsimiles of Richard Woodhouse's Scrapbook Materials in the Pierpont Morgan Library*; vol. 5: *Manuscript Poems in the British Library*; vol. 6: *The Woodhouse Poetry Transcripts at Harvard, a Facsimile of the Wₒpₒ2 Notebook, with Description and Contents of the Wₒpₒ1 Notebook*; vol. 7: *The Charles Brown Poetry Transcripts at Harvard, Facsimiles including the Fair Copy of* Otho the Great. Part 2 of *The Manuscripts of the Younger Romantics: A Facsimile Edition, with Scholarly Introductions, Bibliographical Descriptions, and Annotations*. Gen. ed. Donald H. Reiman. 7 vols. New York: Garland, 1985–89.

————. *The Texts of Keats's Poems*. Cambridge: Harvard UP, 1974.

————, ed. *Twentieth-Century Interpretations of Keats's Odes: A Collection of Critical Essays*. Twentieth Century Interpretations. Englewood Cliffs: Spectrum-Prentice, 1968.

Stonyk, Margaret. *Nineteenth-Century English Literature*. London: Macmillan, 1983.

Strauss, Walter L., ed. *The Intaglio Prints of Albrecht Dürer: Engravings, Etchings, and Dry Points.* 3rd ed. Rev. New York: Kennedy Galleries and Abaris, 1981.

Swann, Karen. "Harassing the Muse." Div. on English Romanticism, MLA Convention. Chicago, Dec. 1985. In Mellor, *Romanticism* 81–92.

Tate Gallery. *The Pre-Raphaelites.* London: Tate and Penguin, 1984.

Thorburn, David, and Geoffrey Hartman, eds. *Romanticism: Vistas, Instances, Continuities.* Ithaca: Cornell UP, 1973.

Thorpe, Clarence DeWitt. *The Mind of John Keats.* 1926. New York: Russell, 1964.

Thorslev, Peter L., Jr. *Romantic Contraries: Freedom versus Destiny.* New Haven: Yale UP, 1984.

Tinker, Chauncey Brewster. *Painter and Poet: Studies in the Literary Relations of English Painting.* Cambridge: Harvard UP, 1938.

Tompkins, Jane P. "The Reader in History: The Changing Shape of Literary Response." *Reader-Response Criticism: From Formalism to Post-Structuralism.* Ed. Jane P. Tompkins. Baltimore: Johns Hopkins UP, 1980. 201–32.

Tooke, Andrew. *The Pantheon, Representing the Fabulous Histories of the Heathen Gods, and the Most Illustrious Heroes. . . .* 1698. 1713 ed. New York: Garland, 1976.

Trawick, Leonard M., ed. *Backgrounds of Romanticism: English Philosophical Prose of the Eighteenth Century.* Bloomington: Indiana UP, 1967.

Trevelyan, G. M. *British History of the Nineteenth Century and After (1782–1919).* 1922. Harmondsworth, Eng.: Penguin, 1979.

Trilling, Lionel. *Beyond Culture: Essays on Literature and Learning.* New York: Viking, 1965.

———. Introduction. *The Selected Letters of John Keats.* Ed. Trilling. New York: Farrar, 1951. 3–41. Rpt. as "The Poet as Hero: Keats in His Letters." *The Opposing Self: Nine Essays in Criticism.* New York: Viking, 1955. 3–49.

Twitchell, James B. "Keats and Cozens: The Systematic Sublime." *Romantic Horizons: Aspects of the Sublime in English Poetry and Painting, 1770–1850.* Columbia: U of Missouri P, 1983. 136–62.

Utley, Francis Lee. "The Infernos of Lucretius and of Keats's 'La Belle Dame sans Merci.' " *ELH* 25 (1958): 105–21.

Van Ghent, Dorothy. *Keats: The Myth of the Hero.* Rev. and ed. Jeffrey Cane Robinson. Princeton: Princeton UP, 1983.

Vendler, Helen. *The Odes of John Keats.* Cambridge: Belknap–Harvard UP, 1983.

Waldoff, Leon. *Keats and the Silent Work of Imagination.* Urbana: U of Illinois P, 1985.

Ward, Aileen. *John Keats: The Making of a Poet.* 1963. Rev. ed. New York: Farrar, 1986.

Wasserman, Earl R. *The Finer Tone: Keats' Major Poems.* Baltimore: Johns Hopkins UP, 1953.

Watson, J. R. "Keats and the Pursuit of the Sublime." *Picturesque Landscape and English Romantic Poetry*. London: Hutchinson, 1970. 141–57.

Webster's Seventh New Collegiate Dictionary. 1965 ed.

Weissman, Judith. " 'Language Strange': 'La Belle Dame sans Merci' and the Language of Nature." *Colby Library Quarterly* 16 (1980): 91–105.

Weisstein, Ulrich. "Literature and the Visual Arts." *Interrelations of Literature*. Ed. Jean-Pierre Barricelli and Joseph Gibaldi. New York: MLA, 1982. 251–77.

Wellek, René. "The Concept of 'Romanticism' in Literary History." *Comparative Literature* 1 (1949): 1–23, 147–72.

———. *The Romantic Age*. 1955. New Haven: Yale UP, 1976. Vol. 2 of *A History of Modern Criticism, 1750–1950*. 6 vols. 1955–86.

White, R. J. *From Waterloo to Peterloo*. New York: Macmillan, 1957.

———. *Life in Regency England*. 1963. New York: Putnam, 1965.

Wilkie, Brian. *Romantic Poets and Epic Tradition*. Madison: U of Wisconsin P, 1965.

Wimberly, Lowry C. *Folklore in the English and Scottish Ballads*. 1928. New York: Ungar, 1959.

Wittreich, Joseph Anthony, ed. *The Romantics on Milton: Formal Essays and Critical Asides*. Cleveland: Case Western UP, 1970.

Wolf, Bryan J. "A Grammar of the Sublime: Or, Intertextuality Triumphant in Church, Turner, and Cole." *New Literary History* 16 (1985): 321–41.

Wolfson, Susan J. "Composition and 'Unrest': The Dynamics of Form in Keats's Last Lyrics." *Keats-Shelley Journal* 34 (1985): 53–82.

———. "Feminizing Keats." *Critical Essays on John Keats*. Ed. Hermione de Almeida. Boston: Hall, 1990. 317–56.

———. "The Language of Interpretation in Romantic Poetry: 'A Strong Working of the Mind.' " *Romanticism and Language*. Ed. Arden Reed. Ithaca: Cornell UP, 1984. 22–49.

———. *The Questioning Presence: Wordsworth, Keats, and the Interrogative Mode in Romantic Poetry*. Ithaca: Cornell UP, 1986.

Woodring, Carl. *Politics in English Romantic Poetry*. Cambridge: Harvard UP, 1970.

Wordsworth, William. *The Letters of William and Dorothy Wordsworth: The Middle Years, Part 2, 1812–1820*. Ed. Ernest de Selincourt. 2nd ed. Rev. Mary Moorman and Alan G. Hill. Oxford: Clarendon, 1970.

———. *The Poetical Works of William Wordsworth*. Ed. Ernest de Selincourt. 5 vols. Oxford: Clarendon–Oxford UP, 1940–49.

Yalouris, Nicholas, ed. *The Acanthus History of Sculpture: Classical Greece*. Greenwich: New York Graphic Soc., 1960.

Zillman, Lawrence John. *John Keats and the Sonnet Tradition: A Critical and Comparative Study*. 1939. New York: Octagon, 1970.

Recordings

Auerbach, Emily, and Joseph Kestner. "John Keats and the Romantic Agony." In *Introduction to Modern English and American Literature I: The Nineteenth Century.* Annenberg-CPB, 0-89776-208-8-C.

Bloom, Claire, et al. *English Romantic Poetry.* Caedmon, TC 3005.

Church, Tony, et al. *John Keats: Poems.* Argo, PLP 1043.

Marcuse, Theodore. *Keats/Shelley.* Educational Audio Visual, LE 7505.

Richardson, Ralph. *The Poetry of John Keats.* Caedmon, TC 1087.

Speaight, Robert. *Treasury of John Keats.* Spoken Arts, SA 868.

INDEX OF NAMES

INDEX OF POEMS BY KEATS

The following is a guide to discussions of, or comments on, the named poems in the "Approaches" section of this volume. For some of Keats's own comments on individual poems, consult the "Subject Index of Keats's Letters" in the "Materials" section.